secrets of a sparrow

Memoirs

secrets of a Sparrow

MEMOIRS

DIANA ROSS

Villard Books
1993
New York

All rights reserved under International and Pan-American Copyright Conventions. Published in the United States by Villard Books, a division of Random House, Inc., New York, and simultaneously in Canada by Random House of Canada Limited, Toronto.

VILLARD BOOKS is a registered trademark of Random House, Inc.

All permissions to reproduce photographs and excerpts from lyrics begin on page 293.

Library of Congress Cataloging-in-Publication Data

Ross, Diana.
    Secrets of a sparrow: memoirs / by Diana Ross. — 1st ed.
      p.   cm.
    ISBN 0–679–42874–7
    1. Ross, Diana.   2. Singers — United States — Biography.
  I. Title.
  ML420.R879A3   1993
  782.42′1644′092—dc20   93–30226
  [B]

Design: Arlene Lee and Jason Cunliffe, Mighty Dimension, Inc.

Manufactured in the United States of America on acid-free paper.
9 8 7 6 5 4 3 2
First Edition

To my children, my husband,
and all those who love me,
even though I really don't want you
to find out who I am
through the words in this book,
I hope that you know who I am
through our time together
and our lives together
and the love that
I feel for you.

Dear Rhonda, Tracee, Chudney, Ross, and Evan,

I always knew I wanted you. Even before I saw your faces, I wanted my babies. You're more than I ever dreamed. Each of you is such a special gift. I hope I've been a good mother and I hope to always be a positive influence in your lives.

I know the difficulties in having a mother that is well known and I know the importance of your individuality and independence.

I want the best for you. I love each of you with all my heart, with all my life. I hope to be here with you a long long time. Hold me, as I hold you, as precious.

My heart is yours,
Mom

I sing because I'm happy,
I sing because I'm free
His eye is on the sparrow
And I know He watches me.

"His Eye Is on the Sparrow"

The human heart has hidden treasures,

in secret kept, in silence sealed.

The thoughts, the hopes, the dreams,

the pleasure, whose charms were

broken if revealed.

Charlotte Brontë, "Evening Solace," 1846

Thank you

Andrea Cagan, Dolores Barclay,
Al Lowman, Diane Reverand,
John Frankenheimer,
Judith Service, Rosanne Shelnutt,
Renee Bell, Quintin Anderson,
Arlene Lee, Jason Cunliffe,
Maddy Miller, Jim Goodkind,
Geneva Saunders, Arthur Fowles,
Ken Johnson, Robert T. Lash,
Sharon Davis, Bob Tuschman,
Dennis Woloch, Maureen McMahon,
Bobbi Hicks.

Without your support and assistance
I couldn't have gotten this done.

CONTENTS

CONTENTS

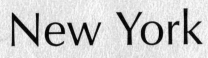

Caught in the Act

It's taken me a lifetime to get here.
I'm not going anywhere!

A t six P.M. on Thursday, July 21, 1983, the weather outside seemed completely calm, but inside my body, I was an electrical force bursting with energy. I wore a multicolored African robe. The opening of the show was to relate to my roots. Pictures of the African jungle were projected on a huge screen, interspersed with images of New York City, in itself another kind of jungle. I stood on the stairs adjacent to the huge platform stage. This was no normal stage; it was a manifested figment of my imagination. And I was about to step into a dream I had spent more than a year conceiving and planning. Thousands of details. It had been grueling, like building a city from scratch. But what a city it was to be! A city of great intensity and light. A city of creativity and vitality. A city that would eventually bring joy to the children. I'm a dreamer. And that's what I did in Central Park. I picked a dream, a goal, and then imagined all the details, drew it up like a blueprint, designed it,

OPPOSITE PAGE:
All our dreams can come true if we have the courage to believe.
The dreamer and the dream become one.

OVERLEAF:
When I ran onstage in Central Park,
I was stepping into a dream.

and then I knew it would happen. I believe that existence is magical, that we can think of something and bring it into being.

The sky looked crystal clear, at least from where I was standing. The sun was heading west and the leaves on the trees lay motionless, the air devoid of even the slightest breeze. The weather was made to order; how could it have been more perfect? The energy in Central Park was electrified, sensual, alive with the heartbeats of the people. I could feel their beauty and excitement. All 400,000 of them. We were gathered together to have a good time, to dance. They wanted to move with me and to allow the music to move through them. I could feel it, and I intended to do my best to give them what they wanted. It was an honor. And, ultimately, my dream of a place in New York City where kids could play would happen. The concert was to be free. We hoped that hats, T-shirts, poster and banner sales could create a sponsorship for a playground, a secure place where children could play, run, laugh, and meet other children, a place to be safe in the magical time of childhood, a wooden playground where little fingers would not get pinched.

ON YOUR MARK.

The African drums started vibrating their compelling beat, the music rose, and the Bernice Johnson Dancers began doing their thing. I couldn't keep my body still; each step that the dancers made reverberated inside of me. I was ready, ready to fly out onstage, ready to dance the dream. I knew that the concert was only a piece of the whole. Most concerts are pure entertainment. Then there are the ones like "We Are the World," which generated tremendous public interest and support to help poverty in the United States and in Africa. Although my concert involved a personal goal, it was not about putting money in my pocket. The concert was merely the vehicle. I was the dreamer. The playground was the dream.

While I straightened the fringes of my jacket, my mind flashed a picture of Belle Isle, a wooden playground of my youth, a sanctuary for my sisters and me when we were young. Whatever else we may have been lacking when we were growing up, this was something we did have, a safe and magical place to play outdoors. Wherever we lived, we always had a playground where there were lots of other children. I wanted this for my own children. I wanted it here in New York City, right here in Central Park. I thought about it all the time. I remember some wise advice: Pay attention to your thinking; what you think about is what you will ultimately become.

GET SET.

The dancers were bending low into the ground, allowing the drumbeats to sail up their spines and to shake through their hips and legs. They were completely connected to the music, in tune with each other and feeding off the energy of the masses of people. These vibrant dancers were young and fresh; they had never been exposed to such powerful charges of energy before. And they knew exactly what to do with it. As I prepared to join them, the wind blew up unexpectedly with such force I feared it might blow the children right off the platform stage. It arrived as if out of nowhere. Then I looked to the side scaffolding where my own children sat and I relaxed as I welled up with pride. My kids were busy flipping their heads all around, trying to count the people in the audience, one by one. My kids were the reason I was standing there, the inspiration for this exciting dream. But I could feel that something strange was about to happen.

What is this feeling I'm having? It must just be the excitement, a little anxiety. Take a deep breath. I'll be all right.

I hoped that nothing would go wrong. I had worked too hard and long to be right where I was, in that moment. My youngest waved to me from the scaffolding. I waved back. That was it.

GO!

I ran out onto the stage. I was there! It was happening! I joined in step with the children. The layers of my robe flew outward, encircling me with vivid color and motion. Oh my God, this was the first moment that I could really see and hear the people. The dreamer and the dream had merged; we were now one. It was an ecstatic union.

In my heart of hearts, I am a dancer. I love to dance and dance and dance until there is no more me. I hid my face beneath the robe, momentarily bodiless, flying around the stage, my fringe shaking. And then it was time. I prepared to shed my multicolored covering. I stood at the back of the stage and allowed the robe sensuously to fall off me. I stepped out of it, revealing my orange sequined bodysuit with a long chiffon scarf attached to the back. Light as air, it clung to me like a second skin. I was there. The protection was gone. Everything felt huge, and I was so small. Now I could really feel the audience. I was ready to take them all into my open heart. I ran to center stage. I was a sleek animal, sensitive and wide open, using my body movements to communicate my joy to the people.

ON YOUR MARK.

GET SET.

GO!

"Hello, New York! You look so beautiful!"

I called out to them. They responded. I was alert; I was certain that I could hear each of their voices. It was daylight; I could see them all clearly, their faces glowing with the ecstatic energy, their hearts wanting to take what I had to give. And I so desperately wanted to give back something to them and to this life that had so blessed me in so many ways.

> *If you need me, call me.*
> *No matter where you are,*
> *No matter how far,*
> *Just call my name,*
> *I'll be there in a hurry,*
> *On that you can depend and never worry.*

I meant that. I really did. I wanted those faces looking up at me to know that I could see them. I always look at their faces. They are the gift and I am the recipient. Come rain or shine. I love the work I do, to sing, to have the opportunity to stand in front of so many and lift my voice. And this was especially true on July 21, 1983, in Central Park.

I don't know how long I had been onstage when the darkness appeared. Time is suspended when I am performing. It wasn't long before that tricky wind blew up again. This time it blew so hard it blew the sun right out of the sky. Everything darkened. Suddenly the sky was completely black, bewildering everyone. From where had the darkness come? It had been cunning like the wind, hiding out. Then the wind came forth in all its glory. It began to whip through the park, thunder crackled, lightning flashed.

My kids! Are they all right? I quickly searched them out in the newly arrived darkness. I breathed a sigh of relief. There they were, still looking fine. Of course they're fine. It's just a little weather tantrum. And then, as if diminished by my logical explanation, the agitated wind encircled me with great force, lifting my diaphanous chiffon scarf up in the air from the floor behind me. I felt as if it were a parachute, that it was about to lift me off the ground. And then the rains came.

"It's all right. We're going to get wet. It's okay. I'm here. It feels good, actually." I allowed the water to caress my body like a lover. I tried to soothe my audience as if they were my children. We were all instantly soaked, but nobody moved. They were here with me. We were all in this together.

"It's taken me a lifetime to get here. I'm not going anywhere. Reach out, hold your hands in the air. Are you afraid of the rain? I won't melt. Will you?" Only the Wicked Witch of the West melted in the rain. I was safe. We all were.

"I've never sung in the rain before." I raised a soaking-wet microphone to my lips and began to sing, "Ain't no mountain high enough. Nothing in this world can keep me from you." Not this rain or anything else. It was my love song to them. The audience had not yet tried to leave; they were getting into the energy; they were dancing in the rain.

I didn't remember the rain in my blueprint, but this was most definitely my dream and here was the rain. I needed to welcome it. I opened my arms wide. I moved them back and forth, arresting any personal resistance that had surfaced. I merged with the pouring water. I let it in. I became a part of it, it became a part of me. Rain and woman were one. Now I was a rain woman. Again, it was an ecstatic union. I was in a wet dream, and it was all right. "This is all right. If we can make this work, we can make anything work, baby."

Everyone looked baffled. What should we do? The entire park was

7

wall-to-wall people. The rain came down like sheets of shimmering glass, creating a rainbow veil. It felt like a dramatic cleansing ritual. I tried to stay open to it.

I looked out once again to find my children, but they were gone. Someone must have taken them to the car. I was relieved they had been rescued. My friend Barry Diller magically appeared beside me. He gestured to me that he wanted me to leave the stage, but I would not. Instead, I took his white jacket, covered my saturated, thin bodysuit, and went back to my post. At this point, I was cold, shaken, yet unmoving. I knew what I had to do. This was my dream, I was the captain, and I would not abandon ship. If I left now, the last lights would go out and the darkness would pose an even greater danger than we already had. I took charge. I would be the last to leave after I was certain that everyone else was safe.

"If anybody wants to leave, do it slowly. Move to your left, and everyone will be all right. The people over here, move to your right. Slo-o-o-wly."

Please, God. Don't let anybody get hurt. I began to silently recite the Lord's Prayer.

> *Our Father Who art in heaven,*
> *Hallowed be thy name.*

The musicians, who were standing in inches of water, began quickly to pack up their instruments. They were trying to avoid getting electrocuted and at the same time trying to save their precious electronic equipment from being ruined by the pelting rain. One of the large floodlights went out. More darkness. I wanted to cry out for help, but no one could hear me. I turned inward.

> *Thy kingdom come.*
> *Thy will be done, on earth, as it is in heaven.*

People were beginning to panic. I heard them screaming that it wasn't safe to stay. I could see that some people were starting to run.

Give us this day our daily bread.
And forgive us our trespasses as we forgive
those who trespass against us.

"Don't push." I spoke with as much assurance as possible. "Stay calm. It's okay. I'm here." As long as they know I'm here, maybe everything will be all right. Soon, it was only me with the piano player, the drummer, and one faithful cameraman covered in a rain cloth. Through the veils of darkness and the relentless rain, I could see only his arm, and he gave me the thumbs-up as if to say, "As long as you stay, so will I." The thunder crackled loudly, and more lights went out. I kept singing, it was my way of keeping everybody safe and getting them out of the park. I was pleading to them for their safety:

> Do you love me?
> Do you love me?
> If you love me
> Get out of the goddamn park!!

I watched everyone leaving and I felt alone, perhaps more alone than I had ever been. There were more than 400,000 people trying to leave the park area. The dream had changed without consulting me. When someone finally dragged me off the stage, I was still pleading for them not to push. Some could hear me, but not everyone, over the rain, the thunder, and the general pandemonium. Most seemed to be having a great time running in the rain. I kept praying for everyone's safety.

And lead us not into temptation,
but deliver us from evil:
For thine is the kingdom,
and the power, and the glory, for ever.
Amen.

I made my way through the crowds of people who were running and falling in the mud. Even then, I tried to keep a happy face, but my tears mixed with the rain and fell to earth, my sorrow and disappointment imprinted in the muddy ground beneath my feet. There was no way out of the park except by foot, so my friend Armando hoisted me up on his back. I was a little girl, riding piggyback on my friend, as we staggered and slipped our way to the street to attempt yet another impossible task: finding a taxi in New York in the rain. The miracle was accomplished. I got home.

Armando left me safely in my suite and went back to do his angel work. He wanted to help the crew save equipment, props, lights, whatever could be saved. I made a quick phone call and learned that my children were safely at home in Connecticut. They had been taken there by friends. Alone in my New York suite, gazing out the window that overlooked Central Park, I stared at one light; it was all that remained of the entire event. Masses of people were spilling out onto every corner of the square around Fifty-ninth Street and Fifth Avenue, running through the rain. Some of them were having fun, goofing and playing with each other in their sudden soggy world. Life goes on. I dropped my head into my hands. What on earth had happened? Where had my dream gone? What happens to a dream when you wake up? Is it gone forever? Does it die off, disappear, and disintegrate into thin air, never to be seen or heard from again? Or does it return to spirit as I think we do, gestating and patiently waiting to be molded back into form by a trusting dreamer who hasn't given up?

I defined a perfect circle as I walked round and round, saying my prayers. I hadn't given up. That's not what I do. The children still needed their playground. I still needed to create it, and create it I would. My clothing may have been saturated, but my determination was not. What happened tonight was not a part of my plan, but sometimes, no matter how intently we make our own plans, nature has its own design. Learning to "let go and let God" has been a tremendous lesson for me.

I kept looking out the window, watching the anonymous people, the people with whom only moments before I had been sharing the same breath. I felt alone and disconnected. I wanted the connection back.

I need to talk to someone, I need to know that everything is all right.

Everything was all right. We repeated the concert the next day. It was hard to put everything back together, the stage, the setting, but Tony Walton did what he could. I searched through my collection of costumes to find something to wear. I ended up with a costume that I had worn before, but it didn't seem to matter. That wasn't what this day was about. It was about overcoming last night and the rain. We were still standing strong.

It's a new day! It's a new day, a beautiful day!

As I ran out onstage, I could see that now, today, it was going to work. The sun was right where it was supposed to be, shining high in the sky. It was beautiful, and all the people were there. It was as if they hadn't left. I looked out at the crowds, and it seemed as if there were even more than yesterday, but who was counting?

11

It's a beautiful day. You're beautiful. I mentioned earlier that the world is watching each of you. You make me so proud. I'm the happiest woman in the world right now, I have a dream come true. I want you to listen to me now. This is being televised worldwide again today. Just calm yourselves. Can you feel me? Yes, this may be the most important moment of my life.

I started to sing one of my favorite songs, "We Are a Family." Its message is one of harmony, of sharing a dream. My thoughts were about us, the family of man, coming together, people holding hands, being one.

The performance was a big success. We all left there in the sunshine, feeling very happy and complete.

The entire concert, along with excerpts from the night before, was simulcast all over the world, and millions of people viewed tapes of my rain ritual. I think they understood. I think it was exciting, full of life and nature and all things real. At first the press wrote sparkling accounts of my experience, revved by sheer excitement. But they soon turned on me with a vengeance, as if I had caused the storm. The rain was my fault, it seemed. Only God has the power to add wind and rain to my dream.

So, building my dream park didn't happen the way I had planned. But build it I did. A playground on West Eighty-first Street in Central Park. There are few people who know, but that's not important. What does matter is that as you read this, children are having fun and running and laughing and safely playing with each other. And their parents can know that while they are there, in that playground of my dreams, they are safe and secure. Come rain or shine.

The Face in the Mirror

I had arrived at the park that day with some degree of anxiety. We were scheduled for a run-through before the actual event, and this was the moment I actually saw the stage that I had danced on so many times in my dreams. My phantom stage, my dream come true. I entered the performance site with great anticipation, but when I looked at it, I was completely taken aback. We had done various drawings and even a mock-up of the actual stage, so I had an idea of what to expect, but these preliminaries had not prepared me for what stood before me. I was in awe; the stage was immense and beautiful. It was so much larger than I had expected, and I must admit that at first impression, it was actually frightening. I walked straight toward it. This was my manifestation. I needed to make friends with it.

I gingerly made my way up the side stairs and walked across the sprung wooden floor to stop motionless in the center of the empty stage. There I stood, a tiny speck of a woman. In front of me was a vast, green, open space, dotted with people relaxing, laughing, and picnicking on the lawn. They were already gathering for the upcoming evening performance; it was truly about to happen. I think there was a part of me that didn't believe it was real, that I was honestly about to do this thing. We had been planning it for so long I had almost lost sight of the fact that this day would ever come. But it had arrived. There was no doubt.

We did a very brief rehearsal. I don't like to do more than that before

OPPOSITE PAGE:
LEFT: At this point, I was cold, shaken, yet unmoving.
I knew what I had to do. I took charge. I would be the last to
leave after I was certain that everyone else was safe.
RIGHT: Central Park, July 22, 1983: It's a new day. It's a new day, a beautiful day!

an outdoor show. I don't like the audience to see too much because I think it removes the element of mystery from the actual performance. As always, we needed to do a sound check and I wanted to test the floor beneath my feet. In this case, we had purposely constructed the stage with a slant, and I wanted to find out if it would be slippery and how it felt to dance on it.

As I moved across the stage, singing a few bars, trying out a few moves here and there, I suddenly got the full impact of the enormous responsibility I had taken on. I had not gotten the sponsorship that I had wanted and not only had I created the dream and would be performing it, but I was also going to pay for it entirely by myself. I had originally thought that I would get Coca-Cola or Pepsi Cola to be my sponsors, or maybe even Steve Wynn from the Golden Nugget in Las Vegas, but none of it had worked out in the end. There were the advertising demands of the soft-drink companies. In order to donate money to lend their names, they would have required massive banners behind my head. That wouldn't work for me, not for this show, and so I decided there might be another way.

Tony Walton, a wonderful designer who worked on *The Wiz*, designed the Central Park set and the large publicity poster. We also had T-shirts, caps, and banners for sale, expensive articles to produce, but it was our intention to get a small return back from each one to begin paying for the playground. As things turned out, we never saw any returns from them; they were mostly destroyed in the rainstorm, along with the booths that we had built to sell these souvenirs. And whatever was left we ended up giving away.

While I was planning and creating the event, I found ways to rationalize the tremendous financial output. I had something very special I wanted to do, this was a rare opportunity for me, and once it was done, everything would work out. I could still try to get some support from either the City of New York or a personal investor to help manifest my dream for the kids. I felt it was such an important and worthy cause. Surely, others would join me in my dream and my efforts. Since commercial sponsorship didn't suit my artistic needs, I would do it differently. I created the Diana Ross Foundation, and whatever funds we were able to raise would go directly to the foundation. From there, I would start building the playground. After all, construction didn't need to begin the day after the performance. Perhaps it would take a year for me to generate the funds and figure out how to proceed. That was okay. All in good time.

For now, I was trying to discipline my mind and deal with each moment as it came up. I took a last look at the expanse of lawn that was continuing to fill up with expectant people. I was grateful that they were there, they looked beautiful to me, and I was already beginning to make contact with them in my own way. As I walked back across the stage, I knew that the next time I stood there and looked out there would be people under the lights. I was overwhelmed with the task in front of me, but for now, I needed to disappear to undergo my transformation, to do my rituals and my preparation to balance and raise up my energy so I could get out there and perform.

As I closed the door to my trailer and shut out the world and the 400,000 people who were already congregating and would be fully gathered when I emerged later, I felt completely alone. It is at this time, before my biggest performances, that I feel more alone than at any other time in my life. I was expecting these feelings, as I know it is a part of the process. And due to the immensity of this undertaking, the isolation was proportionately intense. It had been my decision to do this thing. At the conception of the idea, I had had no clue of how big this production would be, how much it would cost, or how much of a burden the work would become. I guess if we knew the extent of these things when we dreamed them, we might never do them at all.

I never thought it would be easy, but I had been greatly surprised and disappointed by the lack of cooperation I had received. I did know that the decisions along the way would have to be mine. I also knew that I was responsible for the steps to make it all happen, but I did not know that Mayor Koch would be so unpleasant and difficult to deal with. Or that Henry Stern, who was in charge of Central Park, would be unkind to me. I confronted these uncomfortable circumstances, and I forged ahead anyway. Viewing these disappointments as merely obstacles to overcome, I faced each one as it appeared, doing my best. What a famished world we would live in if we only took on what we were certain we could handle!

I slid into my chair in my trailer dressing room and stared at my face in the mirror. All my fears had welled up, and there they were, looking back at me. Well, I had time to deal with them. That was precisely what this time was for. I give myself at least two hours to prepare my mind and my body for each show, to do my makeup, to get into my costume, but mostly I use the time to get my head together, my mind balanced, and my fears in check. I don't know if the general public has any idea about the several hours before a performance, about the tremendous pressure that a performer endures just before he or she is about to drop her normal persona and become vulnerable in front of hundreds of thousands of people.

I probably don't appear shy, but in a way I am. It takes enormous effort for me to prepare myself emotionally for a show, to drum up the courage to walk out onstage and perform. For me, it often takes a degree of courage even to have a business meeting. I believe that I am better emotionally equipped to handle a performance than an intimate business meeting or a one-on-one encounter. In my youth, even my friendships challenged my courage to just be there and be myself. Meetings have always been a terrible burden to me. As I've grown, I've learned some techniques for preparedness that have increased my confidence and enhanced my abilities to deal more comfortably with people in general.

When I have an important appointment coming up, I take some time to visualize the entire exchange from start to finish. I know that there are usually some expectations about what my attitude and thoughts might be, and so often they are wrong. I place myself in readiness for whatever may ensue. I picture all the different possibilities so that I will not be caught off guard. I don't like surprises in these situations.

As a result of my preparations, I have often been seen as more aggressive and stronger than I truly am. I simply appear that way because I already know what I am going to say, and I am so well armored and prepared, it is as if I am about to enter the ring. To some, I probably seem ready to fight, but that's a misinterpretation. I am simply overcoming my insecurities, which I have been dealing with for years and have learned to cover. The older I get, the better it all feels, but letting it just flow is not yet an easy thing for me, and it never has been.

So, that afternoon in the dressing room, I was pacing back and forth, agonizing over the most minute details, and it seemed that everything was off, nothing was right or where it was supposed to be. I found myself yelling at the wardrobe girl unnecessarily for something that seemed quite trivial, like the Q-tips or lipsticks not being in their designated places. It is difficult in a dressing room, when there is so little time to prepare. I don't want to have to search for anything. I want to just reach out and know exactly where it all is: my lipstick, the coffee, the sugar, whatever I need. And so I do a lot of these things for myself, and I take care of my own gowns myself. That's what makes me feel the most comfortable. That way, when I go on, I'm sure.

The stress builds, and no matter what I do, there is no way to stop it. There have been times when my insides were wound up so tight, I felt as if I had forgotten my songs or even the entire show. This has nothing to do with how much rehearsal I've had or how well prepared I am. It's just something that happens, this moment of going totally blank before walking out onstage. I can't think of a more frightening feeling. At times, it happened so suddenly and was so crazy-making, I thought I was losing my mind. It is the weight of the responsibility, the anticipation of the moment when all eyes will be upon me and I must perform well and make it all work.

Relief comes from the crew, the musicians, all of the wonderful people who are there to provide support. And from past experience and training. One of the priceless things that Berry Gordy used to say was, "You have to learn how to think on your feet." He was right. When you're onstage, you have to have your wits about you and be able to react in the moment. If things out of the ordinary happen, and believe me, they often do, like you lose your footing, slip, and fall down or a dress splits up the back, you must be right there and figure out the quickest and most graceful way to handle the situation while standing in front of thousands of people.

Before the Central Park performance, I was so wound up. The pressure was so great, I just sat there at my dressing table, feeling completely untogether, thinking I was scattered all over the place and that I was getting nothing done. You know those dreams when you're running in place as fast as you can, when you're all wound up and getting nowhere fast. That was how it felt, like a frustrating nightmare

19

in which I was moving but standing still. I kept trying to remember what I was going to say and what I was going to do. I read the words of my songs over and over, and as soon as I lifted my head from the paper, I lost them. I remember at one point glancing in the mirror and once again saying to myself, "Will I have to sit in front of this mirror and spend hours putting on makeup for the rest of my life?" This is what I have been doing since I was a child, putting this stuff on my face, then going onstage for two or two and a half hours, maybe three at the most, and then having to undergo the misery of taking it all off again. It's not any fun, but there's no getting around it. The lights do strange things to the skin, and heavy stage makeup is necessary. So when I'm not working, I try not to wear much makeup. Particularly in the daytime.

Having a lot of hair is a huge responsibility, particularly when I'm traveling. It's really quite a job to wash it, brush it, and make sure that I'm not overprocessing it with too much perm or conditioner. In fact, the seemingly simple act of taking care of oneself on the road is actually not simple at all; it is tremendously difficult. There is no time for pampering oneself. And so I have what I call my traveling uniform. This consists of four pairs of black pants and four sweaters, a sweat suit, my favorite jeans, and my cowboy boots. These are things that you don't have to think about—you can just get up, put them on, and you're set for the day. And then I always bring along a great cover-up, a coat or shawl that covers a multitude of sins.

Back to the face in the mirror. Who is this looking back at me? A woman, a mother, who with each stroke of the eyeliner, with each brush of the rouge, is transforming into a stage personality. My shoulders are tense. I breathe deeply, searching for relief from the reality in front of me. My mind wanders to distant places, anywhere but here, away from the pressure. When I travel, I love to be invited to use someone's private plane because that way I can look funky; I don't have to dress up at all. But that isn't always possible. Sometimes I have to walk through public airports where people see me, and there is this expectation that I look a certain way. I have to be Diana Ross, the performer, the star, not Diana, the human being, the mother, the weary traveler. This makes me smile as I write. It is yet another situation where things are not as they appear, where my seemingly glamorous life is really quite difficult.

Anyone who travels knows the inevitable hardships, the airports, the hotels, the bad food. This is a problem when I perform because I have to keep my weight down and avoid all forms of abuse, like having too much to drink and not getting enough sleep. But I do pretty well, as sleeping has never been my problem. As soon as I get offstage and back to my hotel room, I hit the bed. Then in the daytime, I try to keep myself occupied with videos or anything I can find to keep me in the room until it's time for the next show. The only reason I might go out is to see where I am, to take a look at the city and the people. I like to try to know something about the people for whom I am about to perform. I often talk to the limo drivers to get a feel for these things.

And the makeup proceeds. Lining my lips, choosing the perfect colors to blend with the orange of the bodysuit I have chosen for this day. Painting over my lips. Feeling the same anxiety seep back into my body. Using my mind to think about other things that relax me, take me into calmness. Another thing that I like to do when I'm traveling is go antiquing. I love old things, mostly junk. I collect salt and pepper shakers and funky old furniture. Whatever appeals to me at the time. My tastes have changed a great deal over the years. I remember that my mother didn't want to have anything old. In our house there was all this chrome and Plexiglas. I would be out, looking for old couches and funky tables. When I brought them home, Mama would laugh; it tickled her that I would actually spend money on all this old stuff that she'd just thrown away.

I really live a lot less fancy than people imagine. They somehow think that I live in a glass house, but they are forgetting that I am a mother. When you have children, you have dirty carpets, torn-up sofas, and empty walls. I even tape things up around my house, like important messages to myself. I would say that my home feels more like a cozy, loving, living space than anything else. It is warm, comfortable, livable. Although I do have certain areas where I can entertain, this seldom happens. I am a private person living a public life.

I've run out of things to distract me. Eyes done, lips full and blushing. I could pull my hair out of my head by the roots. The fear is spasming through me, and everybody around me is picking it up. I feel

21

as if my lifeblood were draining and I have nothing left to give. How did I get myself into this position? As I look inside, I see that my fears are not about performing. I am a veteran. I have performed too many times before not to trust myself onstage. What I don't trust is the logistics, that everything will pull together and run smoothly. But it is happening, very soon in fact. I have to find a way to trust that it will be all right.

When these kinds of negative thoughts arise, I don't hold on to them very long. This is my discipline because I know how destructive it can be to dwell on them. I often turn on my tape recorder. I have a library of tapes, my tools for inspiration, positive thinking, spiritual reminders. Sometimes before I go onstage, I play some of my past shows to remind myself of things I have said to keep up the vitality and the energy level. These have served me well when I was so exhausted I thought it would be impossible to carry on. There have been those nights when I have been so utterly wiped out that I had no idea where I would find the energy to make it all fresh, real, and brand-new for the audience. But it never fails—no matter how bad the pain, how severe the exhaustion, or how sick I am to my stomach, when I walk out onstage, the pain disappears.

It's the audience. Their incredible energy takes it all away. I have had nights when, as I bent over, all I could feel was the unbearable throbbing in my head. When I lifted myself back up, the feeling of alliance with the audience overcame it all and I went on to perform pain-free. Adrenaline shoots through me during the time I am onstage and acts like anesthesia. Then, the moment I step offstage and stand in the wings, the pain is back full force. But for the time that it's gone, I feel exalted. It's a phenomenon, a state of grace, a blessing from God.

Half hour. Time to get dressed. The final step before show time. I pushed back from my dressing table, stood up, took a last look in the mirror. I'm ready.

Thank you, God, for this wonderful life.
Thank you for your grace and your blessings.
Please keep your eye on this sparrow.

Detroit

Mama, I Miss You

Mama
so beautiful
frightened
thin
good
memorable
my best friend
Mama, Mama
Mama, I miss you.
needing to talk to you.
can you see me?
look at me, Mama.
look.
see how good I am.
I'm a woman now.
I did really good.
look at my babies.

OPPOSITE PAGE:
Mama, I see your face every time I look in the mirror.

OVERLEAF:
Growing up was easy and hard.
Looking back, I don't remember much of the hard times.
I really enjoyed my childhood.

> they're okay
> because of you.
> are you okay?

I don't remember much of my early, early childhood. A photo album helps me feel the time. It's 1947, I was three years old. The pictures cause the memories of my childhood to flood into me through my senses. The disjointed images parade by, dreamlike, surreal, and yet at the same time tangible. I see myself as a small waiflike child with vibrant energy, vital, curious, full of piss and vinegar, and wildly excited to be alive. This picture could be someone else because I don't have it like this in my mind, but I'm told it's me all right. She looks shy, coquettish, sweet, mischievous, happy. Her heart is full and open; she wants life and she wants love. She feels everything, and she misses nothing. I see me running; I loved to run. Feeling like the wind. With wings extended outward, feet planted on the cement below, she flies through space, leaving trails of light behind her. She is fast and elusive, hard to catch or pin down. It is I, the Diana of my youth, second in line in a family of six bursting kids.

> Mama, I miss you
> Mama, what were your dreams?
> what did you wanna be?
> I see you in me
> each time
> I look in the mirror
>
> were you happy?
> were you in pain?
> I wish you were happy
> did I cause you both of these?
> I think I made you happy
> I truly hope so

My mother had an incredible dignity about her. Times were tough, but I never noticed. Growing up was easy and hard. Looking back, I don't remember much of the hard times, and I really enjoyed my childhood. I remember being afraid of certain things, but mostly there was a freedom that I loved. I was a happy child.

5736 St. Antoine between Palmer and Henry, #23. I was born in Detroit. All of us, the Ross family, were born on this street. Barbara Jean was the first. I thought she was the true beauty of the family. We called her Bobbi. I remember loving her, wanting her touch and her warmth, my big sister. She had long pretty hair, she was very smart, and she wore glasses. I was the second child, so as I got older I was always competing with her. I could sing and dance better than she could. I was stronger, and I was very fast. I could really run fast. I loved to swim. I remember Mama would come to watch me swim, and she used to think I looked pretty in the water because everybody else would be gasping for their breath and I would just stroke smoothly along. I think the swimming team must have been hard for Bobbi because her thick, long hair took so long to dry. I wanted my parents to like me as much as they liked her. I thought they liked her best, so I would do other things to get their attention. I'd try to entertain the family and see if I could bring a little joy into their lives, especially when I knew that they were unhappy. I would try to do everything the best, better than Bobbi, so Mama and Daddy could see me. I was never afraid to stand up in front of my mother's friends and entertain them. Do a little tap dance or even sing "Your Cheatin' Heart."

Then Rita was born. She had lots of allergies, which caused her to scratch herself, and her skin would swell up from certain foods. Everyone tried to take care of her. She was the baby now—not me. I was the big girl. Even with her allergies, Rita was pretty, with gray eyes and beautiful hair. My brother Fred was the first son, so they gave him Daddy's name, Fred Earl Ross, Jr. Arthur was next, such a tiny boy; he was called T-Boy. And finally, Wilbert Alex Ross was the last son; he was called Chico. That was us, the Rosses.

27

It's good you're not here now.
it's all gone wrong.
T has troubles.
Chico can't get it together.

Rita's sometimes sad.
Bobbi is full of life and moving on
just like me
strangely driven by we don't know what

can you see me Mama?
can you hear me?

We were a handful for Mama, but we knew that she loved us completely. We all knew that. Mama is gone now. She died October 9, 1984.

Mama, Mama, Mama can you hear me?
Mama I miss you

For two long years, Mama suffered terribly. It seems unfair that she should have left this life in such pain. She was kind, loving, and giving. She had been bothered by something in her chest for some time, but she had kept it to herself. That was Mama's way. She didn't want to trouble anyone. We took her to the doctor as soon as we knew, but it had gone too far; it was breast cancer. She had a mastectomy and then chemotherapy. The chemo was what seemed to take the life out of her. That was when she became thin and drawn.

In two short years, the change happened. It was fast and traumatic for all of us. She took whatever medications we gave her. We could see that she was trying to hold on to life, but we could also see that the life was slowly leaving her.

During the last months of my mother's life, I was booked into Radio City Music Hall, one of the most demanding jobs I have ever done. She became weaker with each day, and I began flying back and forth, completely torn between my career commitments and my mother, whom I loved more than anyone else. My life had become a nightmare; I wasn't completely present for my work or for my mother.

In the last days of my mother's life, she did not want to lie down. She wanted to walk around, to take tiny steps, to rock herself gently. I felt what she wanted, and I understood. I showed the nurses how to support her. Mama would place her hands on their shoulders to balance herself, and they would hold her waist while she moved around, touching things she remembered. It was as if she were in a silent battle with death and refused to give in.

I finally got my dear loving housekeeper, Geneva, to go there to be with her. I trusted Geneva. She really took care of my mother in those last days, those last hours. We all did as much as we could; we tried to soothe her pain, but there was little that could be done. Mama had tried to protect me from my pain all my life, and now that she was suffering, I felt so helpless. I would hold her as much as she would let me. That was my way of letting her know how much I loved her. There was no time for talking, and even if there had been, words would have been meaningless.

I was in a race against time. I would close the show in New York, jump on a plane, fly to Detroit, stay with Mama all day, jump back on a plane, and open the show the next night. I can't remember when I slept or ate. It was so very hard, the pressure, the exhaustion, the responsibility. At Radio City, I was in such grief and was so distracted. The audience can never, never know what is happening in a performer's life, and I was not open to talking about my pain. It was private, and at that time I found it very hard to talk about it. Mama was foremost in my mind. I tried to hold back my tears. I tried to be strong for her and the rest of the family. It was a tremendous strain. In hindsight, I wish I had canceled those shows and been completely there for my mother, even though there were lots of other caregivers like Aunt Bea and my sisters. I would have been happier today if I had been there all the time. When things are actually happening, it isn't always easy to know what's right. I can count on my fingers the number of times I have canceled engagements or shows. Even though I am facing a great personal tragedy, I refuse to back out of an engagement. It has always been very important

29

for me to keep my word. If I say I am going to do something or be somewhere, you can count on it. Integrity and honesty form the bookends of my life. Trying to do the right thing for everybody else and losing sight of my own needs is part of my problem in life.

I was about five steps away from my mother when she passed. Where does life go, so vibrant and full in one moment and in the next moment gone forever? I know she is here with me and I am with her. I wish she and I had talked more, about her hopes and dreams, about who she really was. At first I felt strangely angry when my mom died. I hadn't had a chance to give her all the things and the kind of life she deserved. She had worked so hard for us. Given up her dreams for her six children.

The space my mother occupied in my heart and in my life is empty now. I feel the loss, the ache. We are never prepared. Through that loss, I am reminded of the importance of health, a secure financial future, spending time with family and those you love—friends, people, teaching our babies.

> did she give up?
> did she just get so tired
> she didn't want to fight anymore?
> Mama, I miss you.
> I wish you could see my kids.
> Rhonda's graduating from college.
> Tracee wants to be in fashion —
> wonder where she got that
> Chudney's going to college
> and my boys, Mama — I finally got my boys
> I didn't think it would happen
> and I'm happy — as happy as I can be
> as happy as I know how to be,
> in the pursuit of happiness but
> I'm closer than I ever was — I think

Rhonda with her grandmother Ernestine.

A Quiet Force

I was such an energetic child that I don't think Daddy ever quite knew how to deal with me. And I didn't know how to deal with him either.

When I met my father, I was two years old. It was the day he returned from the army. I was a baby when he left, so he was a stranger to me by the time he was discharged. When he stood before me, he was a looming figure towering over me, like a giant with his head nearly up against the ceiling. He was very tall.

Daddy. I wanted to be my father's special girl. I was always looking for signs of love and approval in his eyes. He was smart, proud, confident, refined, respectful. He had the benefits of his striking physical presence. Emotionally miles away, Daddy was a quiet man who didn't talk a lot to anyone. I never succeeded in making that deeper emotional connection with him. I don't want to keep reenacting old scenes and reliving the pain this distance caused, but I grew up wanting his love, wanting affection from him. Since he just wasn't the type to give those things, I mostly tried to keep away from him. He was very attractive, but still there was this distance. It was as if I could stand right beside him and put out my hand, yet he remained just beyond my reach. No matter how long my arms grew, no matter how far I reached toward him, I could never get close enough to touch him, and I'm not sure why.

OPPOSITE PAGE:
What a beautiful couple.
I can feel my parents' love here.
It's wonderful to come from love.

He seemed silent. I don't remember a lot of laughter or sharing of affections. No hugs or kisses. Always saying no when I asked him for something. Can I . . .—NO—almost without thinking. As I got older, I always tried for his approval and his attention, but he mostly seemed preoccupied and busy. He was there, but not there.

Maybe a lot of kids grow up afraid of their fathers for many different reasons. Maybe because he's big. Maybe because he's strong. Maybe because he speaks in a loud voice or wears big shoes.

Maybe he was afraid. Did daddies have fear? I never thought so. I thought fathers were too big and strong to have fear. Maybe there was nothing at all. Maybe Fred Earl Ross, Sr., was just that way. I don't know.

Daddy was a hardworking man. We didn't have a lot when we were growing up, but everybody that we knew was poor as well so we didn't feel as if we had any less than anybody else. In fact, we all had about the same, but since Daddy worked so hard, it sort of seemed as if we had a little bit more. He worked two and sometimes three jobs to support us. He worked at Meyers and Stock suitcase factory, the gas station, the post office, and American Brass, just to name a few. Throughout my childhood, he stayed unreachable, and in certain ways, he still is. I guess my arms never did grow long enough.

To this day I wish I knew him better. He doesn't talk much about things. I wonder if my brothers and sisters felt as I did. I tried not to get in his way; I hoped I didn't have to.

Our relationship has grown over the years. I now understand him better. He is a shy man who feels things very deeply. He finds it very hard to express these feelings, and he has never asked for anything. I know he loves his family dearly and has really tried to be there for us through all of our ups and downs. It's nice to take time and rethink your childhood memories. It would also be nice just to sit and talk to our loved ones to get a better understanding of their hopes and dreams. I cherish my father. I'm happy that he is still with us. I know that his strength and quiet force has helped shape my life in ways that I may never be able to express.

The model for what I want in my husband must not be molded by my childhood hurts but by my understanding of life as an adult. I see my painful experiences in life as stepping-stones.

I am passionately expressing my parents.

Sweet Like Jelly

As untouchable as Daddy was, Mama was the opposite. She was all heart. A warm, soft, loving woman. Mama was my heroine. I thought that heroines weren't supposed to get sick and leave their babies. No matter who you are, you're never really prepared for a loved one to leave. I loved her so much. I wanted her to be here for a long time, to watch me blossom, to know my joys and my sorrows. To share my successes with me, to see me as an adult, to watch my girls grow up and to play with my baby boys. That didn't happen. I think of her every day. She lives inside of me as a warm, sweet longing. I remember her beauty, her zest for life. Her love lies at the foundation of my life. Her goodness almost defies description, as bright as the sunlight that poured in through her yellow kitchen windows, as sweet as home-cooked jelly. Her love gave me strength.

When the jelly is cooking, it gives off a sweetness that is so intoxicating you can practically eat up the air. When Mama and my Aunt Bea made jelly, they did it in our kitchen, maybe because it was so filled with sunlight. I would sit at the kitchen table, sniffing and drinking in the heady aroma.

I remember the day Mama, Aunt Bea, and some of the neighbors were making jelly. Aunt Bea was Mama's sister, and she was like a second mother to us. Mama was the youngest of twelve kids, and Aunt Bea was right in front of her. My mother's mother, Grandma Moten, named her Virginia Beatrice, but she was always Aunt Bea to us. Vir-

OPPOSITE PAGE:
Aunt Bea was Mama's sister, and she was like a second mother to us.
(left to right: Ernestine, "Uncle" Underwood, Aunt Bea)

ginia and Ernestine, my mama, were inseparable; they had come to Detroit together. Although they were as close as sisters could be and really loved each other, you could never tell that to look at them; they spent so much time arguing and bickering. We always said they were like chalk and cheese. Mama seemed to be sick a lot. I didn't know then that she had TB, but whenever she went into the hospital, which happened often, Aunt Bea took over and cared for us. We even went to the South once to stay with one of Mama's other sisters, Aunt Willie, when Mama was hospitalized.

"Don't come too close now," Mama warned me. "And don't shake the table. The jelly will spill, and it's hot." And guess what happened? I did it. I shook the table. I hadn't meant to do it. It was an accident. I always tried to be good and please Mama. The scalding sweet fruit syrup splattered on my exposed skin. As if paralyzed, I watched it sail through the air, saw it land on my arms and legs like long streaks of purple embers. I couldn't get out of the way fast enough. I'm burned, I thought. I'm in trouble. Then I waited. At first, I felt nothing, but then the pain throbbed straight through me. It was excruciating. The quiet, contented sound of a lazy afternoon, of women's light laughter and easy gossip, was instantly transformed into a frenzy of motion. Each neighbor rushed to her respective apartment, returning with all manner of assorted oils, ointments and butters, medicines and remedies to rub all over my blistering body. I lay there and let them minister to me while I counted the throbbing pains that coursed through me. I hoped my mother and Aunt Bea wouldn't be too angry at me. They weren't; they cared for me tenderly, and I healed. I hadn't been severely burned. I was okay. Mama just looked at me with that "I told you so" look and shook her head.

Mama was always concerned that I was messing up something. In her letter written May 20, 1957, from Bessemer, Alabama, her last line was

We'll see you all soon. I hope Diana has been a good girl.

Mother

38

1617-19 Street
Bess, Ala
May

Dear Bob Diane
& Fred & Arthur.

We're having a very
nice time, but I'm tired
out at nite for the baby
keeps me running all
day to keep him out of things
when I sleep I sleep. he
sleeps with me a nights
and he doesn't wake until
break fast no bottle all
night.

I'm over to missie and
I can't keep him out of the
road he won't stay in the
yard for the grass is
lovely. I'm having a lovely
time. Dorthey & Dorlyn With
an missie are jeenny to that
feel the boy chier, rides

their wagon. you should
see him now that he
needs a hair cut. (too) (bad)
will see you all soon
I hope Diane live leen
a good girl. Mother

Miss Barbara J. Ross
635 Belmont
Detroit 2, Mich.

5736 St. Antoine

My neighborhood, or shall I say my world, was two blocks long: a playground, backyard, porches, fences, alleys. I don't remember trees. I remember telephone poles that I wanted to climb as I got older. I wanted to show how tough I was. I was never afraid.

We lived in a big apartment building with lots of units. 5736 St. Antoine. I used to fly up the stairway, skipping steps, racing against myself, each time seeing how quickly I could get to the third floor, where we lived. On the first floor on the right, I passed the Watleys' place. I saw them once, and then I can never remember seeing them again. On the second floor, I ran by the Tolbridges, Dorothy and Anna, Johnny, Brenda, and Pat. Their apartment was on the right. To the left were Thelma Lee and Ed Washington. One more flight up, us, the Rosses. We were on the right-hand side. On the left was Mrs. Marshall, an old woman from Jamaica.

5736 St. Antoine, #23. I can clearly see the number of the building. But even in my most vivid memory, as I stand in front of our front door, I cannot see the apartment number. Whenever I walked into the living room, the dark green walls with bright white trim comforted me. I loved sitting on the big, soft burgundy sofas, the ones that enveloped my small body as I sank down into the center. I used to stick my fingers down in the dark creases of those sofas when I was alone and pull out lost pennies, abandoned keys, and money that had dropped out of grown-ups' pockets. I was a lucky kid. I could always find money.

OPPOSITE PAGE:
I'm the one with the big bow.

We were a family that loved music; this narrow living room with windows that looked out on to an alley contained both a radio and a record player, one of which was usually turned up. To the left was a fairly open room with French doors, a nice-sized room that was my parents' bedroom. It had their things, their smell, and it always seemed so huge to me. Years later, when I heard that the building was about to be demolished, I went back to see it one more time. I felt like a child again when I knocked on the door and asked the people who were living there if I could walk through just once. I felt so sad because Mama and Daddy's smell was gone and everything was so much smaller, as if it had shrunk.

The bedroom must have been too small for Mama because she put up a long metal rack in the hallway and hung her clothes there. The rack was visible from my bed, so while I lay there trying to fall asleep, my mind played scary tricks on me as it turned the clothing into bizarre shapes and silhouettes. I used to hide under the covers because I thought strange people were standing right there in the hall, looking into my room and watching me sleep. I shared my bedroom with my sisters. In this room, we giggled, cried, fought, played, and grew up together. But I didn't like it at night.

Continuing down the hallway, just before we reached the kitchen, there was another smaller hallway that led straight to the bathroom. The bathroom had a mystery, a big hole in the door just beneath the knob. I don't know how it got there, but my memory whispers something about someone kicking in the door. I think it was Daddy.

At the far end of the hallway was the hub of our life, the bright yellow kitchen that Mama loved so much, that we all loved so much. When I first moved to California, I had my own kitchen painted yellow. I guess I wanted to be like Mama. In many ways I still do, and in many ways I am like her.

The back door of the kitchen led onto a small porch that overlooked the backyard, the place where we liked to play. There is nothing that sounds quite like the clinking and snapping of marbles when you get a hit, and nothing like the silence when you miss. I wonder if kids today play games like we did? I suppose they must, but I never see them.

42

We played so many wonderful games. I remember our vibrant, high-pitched, childish voices calling back and forth in my favorite circle game:

> *Who stole the cookie out of the cookie jar?*
> *Not I stole the cookie out of the cookie jar!*
> *Then who stole the cookie out of the cookie jar?*
> *Number One stole the cookie out of the cookie jar.*
> *Not I—*

(and on and on and on.)

Everybody took a turn. You miss, you're out! We lived for the summers when we could be outdoors, when the days were long and even after dinner we could play outside as long as there was light to see each other. We played root the peg, a game where you used a knife to mark the earth. Mama made sure we only used a kitchen knife, nothing too sharp, anything with a point would do, something that we could stick in the dirt. And there were so many more. We had great games. We laughed hard, and we played hard. We were always outside.

The sound of silence. I liked riding my bike to Belle Isle all by myself, just gliding down the streets, full of mischief, feeling free. My two-wheeled bike offered a freedom only the wind knew. In these moments, the whole world was shiny. It's not that Detroit was a beautiful city; it was not. But for me, it had a feeling that was beautiful. All in all, I had a good childhood, and freedom was a large part of it. I loved being alone somewhere, searching the sidewalks for lost change. There's a dime; there's a nickel. It must be my lucky day. I was always lucky, and I knew it. The streets and alleys were fascinating places to explore, not dangerous as they are today. Or if they were, I didn't know it. To me they were a delight.

Mostly we played hard and we laughed hard and we came in at night, wired and then quickly exhausted, ready to drop off into the sleep of a satisfied child. My memories are ones of great joy, shared love, and spirited play, but it wasn't all like that. There was some fighting, too.

43

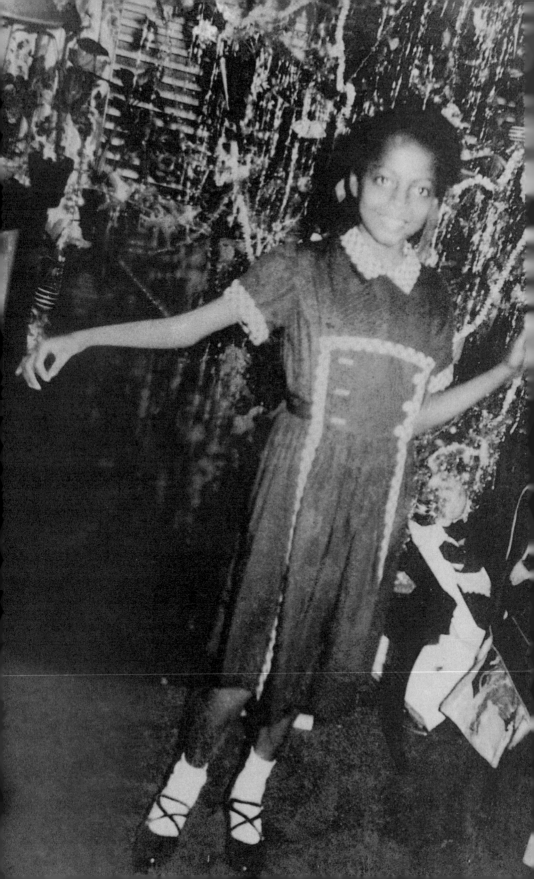

A Bad Dream

O ne night, I woke up in bed, not sure if I was asleep or awake, lost in that space that only exists at dawn or deep in the night, just before awakening. I must have been no more than six years old, and with my eyes half closed, I followed the muffled sounds of crying. Something was wrong. It was Mama. I softly said, "Mama?" but there was no answer. Surely these sounds were not coming from my mama. She was strong, the strongest woman I had ever known. She yelled, scolded, laughed, and sang. She didn't cry.

"Is everything all right, Mama? Where are you?"

"Go back to sleep now."

I persisted. The cries were coming from somewhere in the room. Was it Mama? Where was she? I couldn't see her in the darkness, but my heart said I must do as she says. I was frightened. I can still feel the knot in my stomach. What in God's name was wrong? Only for a moment, I thought she had stopped. So I said again, "Mama, please can I come to you?" "Quiet! Don't let him know I'm here. If he finds me I don't know what he'll do! Go back to sleep, baby, go back to sleep."

I didn't see Mama's face that night, but I will never forget how she sounded, how she felt. I don't know what in the world Mama could have done wrong. To a little girl, this was very upsetting, and today I never knew what her sorrows and pains might have been. She didn't reveal much of her problems to me. I only knew that Mama was not happy,

OPPOSITE PAGE:
All in all I had a good childhood, and freedom
was a big part of it. I was lucky, and if I have any bad
memories, I hope they're not true.

so I always blamed Daddy for their problems. I don't think they were very happy.

I cried that night, but I didn't make another sound. Sleep didn't come quickly. I don't know how long I was awake, but the rest of the night was quiet. No more crying, no more fighting or yelling. I just didn't understand. In the morning, it was all over, like a bad dream, as if it never really happened. Mama was just the same as she was any other morning, but she avoided my eyes. We never spoke about it. I was too young for Mama to tell me the truth, but after that, whenever I woke up at night, I thought I heard her cry. I hope these memories are not true.

Trácee with her grandmother Ernestine.

Just Let Yo' Ole Curtains Burn Up!

A unt Bea, just like Mama, was always there for us. She couldn't have been more devoted if we had been her own children. As far as I can remember, Aunt Bea always lived with us or at least nearby. She was our second mom. She had a boyfriend for a long time named Underwood, but she never married him and she never had any children of her own. It seemed that she basically gave up her life to take care of us, her sister's children. I wish I had talked more to her and Mama about their lives. She died one year after Mama did. I miss them both terribly. They spent so much time in Mama's kitchen, cooking and bickering and being family.

One day, the apartment nearly burned up, and it all started in that kitchen. Fire from the stove shot up the kitchen curtains, and they exploded into flames. Just like that. It was an accident. Aunt Bea wasn't around then; she must have been living separately from us at the time. Bobbi, Rita, and I were sitting together at the kitchen table, the sunshine pouring in the window beside the stove. We were eating or playing, doing what sisters do in yellow, sunlit kitchens in the afternoon, waiting for some savory-smelling dish that was cooking on the stove. Mama was a great cook, and the aroma of her food always meant warmth and security. Suddenly the heat rose, the white cotton curtains turned bright red and orange and began to crackle. They were on fire.

My sisters and I darted into the next room where Mama was washing

OPPOSITE PAGE:
My story has often been referred to as "rags to riches,"
but in truth, the Rosses were never raggedy.

the floor. Mama always kept our small space immaculate. Cleanliness was important, protecting ourselves from the bugs and the rats.

"Mama, come quick," we all shouted at once. "Come see what's happening in the kitchen. Come quick!"

Mama looked up at us, instantly wearied by our bursting energy. "Now, girls. I'm busy. Go back and—"

"But Mama, Mama. Hurry, now!"

Her voice became more stern. "Can't you see I'm busy? Now leave me alone. I'm trying to finish this—"

"Okay then, Mama," I interrupted her. "Just let yo' ole curtains burn up! See if I care."

She flew past us. We were very scared, and we huddled in the far corner of the kitchen away from the scorching heat. I never saw Mama move so fast; she was all arms. I can still hear the smacking sounds that the towel made as she hit the fire with it over and over. The bright orange fire soon became gray smoke. The succulent smell of savory fried chicken became the acrid stench of burning pots and smoke-damaged, drenched cotton. Things happen fast sometimes. Mama was furious, but she didn't have anybody to blame. Aunt Bea wasn't there.

Most of the time Mama and I were very close. I always wanted to be a good girl. I think I was. I wanted Mama to be proud of me; I wanted to be her best helper. I think I was. Of course, to hear Bobbi tell it, I didn't help out at all, but she was wrong. I didn't mind helping in any way I could. Doing chores was a way to get Mama's approval. So I cleaned the chitlins for dinner. And I ironed the sheets. There were no permanent-press sheets in those days and I didn't really like ironing, but I did it for Mama. I fell into a rhythm; I gave the job life and threw myself into it. I made the whole thing into a dance and a sing-along.

> *Fold it first.—Hit it.*
> *Do the top.—Hit it.*
> *Turn it over.—Hit it.*
> *Do the back.—Hit it.*
> *The heat pours through.*
> *Then start again.*

I danced my way through it. No wasted movements. Fast. That's how I did it. That was me. Mama used to look at me with a big smile on her face and say, "You're so fast, if you're not careful, you're gonna get pregnant before you're grown." She always said these things with a big broad smile. I loved it when she smiled; it always made me smile, too. She made me feel loved and secure. Of course there were many things that, as a child, were hard for me to understand, but I know that with my childlike innocence the world was beautiful and I liked being there.

Big-Screen Magic

Mama used to do odd jobs to help support the family. On Saturday mornings, she worked at a movie house. It was called the Regent. We kids took turns accompanying Mama there. I thought it was a very special thing that she did, and I felt so lucky when she would take me with her. Mama and I would get up early in the morning, before the rest of the world stirred, and walk a long way to get there. It was the most magical place in the world. When we got there, the theater was empty. It was scary. When we stepped inside the darkened theater, I would stand at the front of an aisle, in awe of the emptiness in front of me. I would walk down the aisle and choose any seat I wanted. I felt alone and tiny. I remember sitting in a seat and watching the movie. It must have been a Saturday because I didn't have to go to school.

Mama would bend over and disappear behind this big blaring machine they called a blower. Starting at the back of the theater, she would reach the arm of that angry contraption under each of the seats and blow out all of the trash. She worked fast and hard, making her way up and down every row, never missing a plastic cup or a piece of trash. Mama never really looked up; she always worked bending over. Then she collected all that stuff into a huge pile and put it outside in the monstrous Dumpsters that stood out back. There was an awful lot of work and I tried to help, but soon the projectionist would arrive and start playing that day's movie while Mama was still working. Mama just kept blowing

OPPOSITE PAGE:
Blacks didn't show up much in films at that time, but I wasn't aware of color. I was simply lost in a magical, emotional world of joy, tragedy, and laughter.

that trash, and I got to watch the show. I was instantly mesmerized, even though it was hard to hear the voices over the sound of the blower and even though the projectionist sometimes just showed parts of the movies. None of that mattered. I felt it was all for me. As soon as the picture was projected on the screen, I was in the movie, inside the story, up on the big screen. Magic. I liked them all, westerns, love stories.

Blacks didn't show up in films at that time except maybe as slaves or maids, but I was too young to notice such things. I wasn't aware of color; I was simply lost in a magical, emotional world of joy, tragedy, and laughter. I thought it was funny when a character opened up his eyes real wide and said, "Yassuh, Boss." I didn't know that when I laughed at him, I was laughing at myself. For me it was a time of freedom, youth, and innocence.

Fred Ross, Sr.

A Wailing Night

We played endlessly in the backyard of 5736 St. Antoine, just behind the back doorway of our kitchen. I used to sit on a stool in that doorway, particularly in the summer, with the warm sun shining on my face. I picture myself in something red, maybe some red pants. No, it must have been a red dress because I can still feel that scratchy screen door lying against my skinny naked leg on a beautiful summer's day. The yard wasn't soft and green like grass. It wasn't really even a yard. It was hard and gray; it was concrete, but we played there anyway. Beneath that yard, there was a strange little recessed area, also concrete, that always smelled like pee. We stayed away from that underneath part, but we played up above. I went back to the building site after it was torn down and collected some of the bricks. Just to remember.

Whenever I think about the stoop out in front of our building, I am haunted by the vision of one of our neighbors, a poor woman, a mother, who sat out there all night long wailing. I can still hear the sounds she made, the sobbing and screaming all through the night. Everybody let her cry. I lay beside Bobbi in the double bed and we put our hands over our ears to block out the sound, but it didn't work. Nothing would drown out her agony. She was all I could hear. I didn't sleep that night. Neither did Bobbi. Nobody in our building did.

This woman's two children had been playing next to a big refrigera-

OPPOSITE PAGE:
My memories are ones of great joy, shared love,
and spirited play—and some fighting, too.
I love my brothers and sisters.

tor. It had been abandoned out on a back porch of the building across the street. The kids climbed inside. There was an older boy who was playing with them. Maybe it was hide-and-seek, nobody knows exactly, but somehow the refrigerator door got closed on them. It was said that he had meant to open it up again and let them out, but he got bored with the game. While they hid, he just forgot about them. They were locked in. By the time they were found, it was too late. They were dead. When we heard about it, nobody knew what to do. The mother could not be comforted. I was young but not too young to feel the pain. This was my first experience of the death of someone I knew. We used to play with those children, and now they were dead. I understood that a mistake had been made that was beyond correction. I felt the sense of helplessness and deep grief that accompanies death. I wondered what it was like for those kids. As a kid myself, all I could think about was how long it took for them to die, if they screamed and if it hurt very much. These were new thoughts and feelings for me, new confusions. I still don't like to think about it. It remains a part of the memories of my childhood, inextricably woven into the foundations of that apartment building, a phantom that long after the building was demolished still lives on.

Fighting Back

Growing up in the fifties was a time of great excitement for blacks. It was about Joe Louis winning, and when he did, we all won. We, the Negro people, as we called ourselves then, all desperately needed to win. We were fighting for our self-esteem in order to feel good about ourselves, in order to feel a sense of our freedom.

I was a tough kid, a tomboy. "Don't fight," Mama would tell me. "When bad things happen, just walk away. Stay away from trouble-makers. They have nothing to do with you." I did as she said. I wanted to do what Mama said and be a good girl.

One day when I was eight years old, I came home from school in tears. My face was red, and I was terribly beat up. I finally told Mama that a kid had slapped me in my face. At her past advice, I had walked away.

She stroked my burning cheek. "What did they call you?" she wanted to know.

"They called me 'nigger,' Mama."

Mama's face went cold, and she was really mad. "Don't you ever let anybody hit you in your face and call you a nigger. Yes, you hear me. I mean for you to fight, fight for all you've got. You know I have never told you to fight before, but I want you to fight for your dear life. Never let anyone make you feel bad about who you are."

I was puzzled by her words. Did she really mean what she was saying, or was I misunderstanding her? She went on as if she could read my mind. "Oh, yes. You're hearing me right. And I don't mean just fight either. You'd better win. Because if you don't win, when you come back here, I'm gonna whip your butt."

One week later, Mama was wiping blood from my nose and washing my bruised face. I had been in a fight, and I couldn't say that had I won. I was ashamed, angry, and confused all at the same time. I stood there with my eyes not blinking, looking up at Mama. I wasn't sure what was right. I half expected her to be angry at me because I had always been told not to fight, but she wasn't angry.

It had happened in the school. Everything felt dusty and dirty that afternoon. Some kids were picking on me and had called me a name, a bad name, and then they giggled and ran away. I knew that they were trying to make me feel bad about myself, but I didn't. I just felt angry, and I had hauled off and swung at them. They had hit me back twice and scratched my face before they took off running and laughing.

Sticks and stones may break my bones,
But names will never hurt me.

I picked up my schoolbooks and started walking. By the time I reached home, I had made a decision. From now on, I would fight back and just as Mama said, I would win. I had to. I would never come home with my face all scratched up again. No more bloody noses. I had decided this but not because of what Mama said. I made the decision for myself this time. I was never going to let anybody put me down again. It was important for me to be strong and to fight back.

That was a turning point. Somewhere I promised myself that from then on I wouldn't cry very much. If someone hit me, I got really tough and up in their face. In fact, I began to protect my two sisters, especially Bobbi, the older one. I never let anyone pick on her or on Rita. And they usually didn't because they knew they would have to answer to me. I may have been skinny, but I was tough, wiry, fast, and strong. I was never going to let anybody put me down.

Although I had moved myself into the position of family protector against anyone on the outside, Bobbi and I used to fight with each other.

One day, I hit Bobbi hard and then she hit me back. I have no recollection of what set us off, it could have been just about anything, but I was better at fighting than she was. I certainly had more practice. I made her so angry that day she ended up throwing Ajax cleanser in my face. I went running to Mama. Tattling was unusual for me, but I had been humiliated. With the caustic white cleanser still all over my face, I held the empty Ajax container up in front of me and sobbed, "Bobbi just hit me and put this in my face." Mama looked at me, laughed, and asked, "Why didn't you hit her back?" I walked away shattered and completely puzzled again. I guess there are some things you fight for and some things you don't.

Point of Origin

I Sing Because I'm Happy

There's nothing like waking up Sunday morning to the sound of someone singing, humming, or whistling. It's a lovely sound to hear first thing in the day, a new day.

My mother always sang around the house. Sometimes she hummed or whistled. My father whistled also. Mama used to sing a very moving spiritual called "His Eye Is on the Sparrow":

> *Why should I feel discouraged*
> *And why should the shadows come?*
> *Why should my heart feel so lonely*
> *And long for heaven and home?*

Mama would hum or sing these words till I remembered them well. The words are haunting, sad, and when Mama passed away, I had it sung for her this last time. Her favorite tune is so much a part of me:

> *I sing because I'm happy,*
> *I sing because I'm free.*
> *His eye is on the sparrow*
> *And I know He watches me.*

OPPOSITE PAGE:
This was a magical time.

OVERLEAF:
I was so happy finally to return to my roots and share the experience with my husband and my kids.

I was Mama's little sparrow because I was quick and thin and loved to sing. My body felt light as a bird, and I would imagine that I could fly away wherever I wanted to go. Freedom was what the sparrow meant to me: freedom, sensitivity, and delicacy.

Mama would sing while she was doing the housework, cooking, cleaning, ironing, or when we walked to church. It was her favorite song. There was a sweetness to Mama's voice. It was high-toned, but there was a soul in there that felt so vulnerable and strangely sad. It was inside her, inside her chest—a sound that gave you goose bumps. My mother had a gospel voice, and she sang "His Eye Is on the Sparrow" in a loving tempo, very slow.

Have you ever been to church and heard someone sing something that gave you chills—a gospel choir singing "Ave Maria" or a beautiful hymn? That's how my mother's voice made me feel.

"His Eye Is on the Sparrow" always had great meaning for me. It talks about how God protects all his creatures, even his littlest ones. I think in a sense it was my mother's prayer or her protection for us. She protected us from many things in life, trying to shield us from its harsher realities. We never turned our backs on adversity but used the pain in life to learn from, to grow, and to move on to brighter times.

I've always looked at the more positive side of things. All the pain I've had in my life, I'll hold on to it for a second and then I'll let it go. I really try to let go of all the negativity and leave the rest up to God. That's one of the beautiful gifts my mother gave me, the ability to allow certain things to be.

Mama gave this song to me, and I am blessed in my life. I feel watched over and protected and loved and taken care of in my life. This is my prayer, and I'm so thankful every minute of the day.

My childhood gave me the greatest gift available: my profound spiritual faith, a faith that has been simple and unwavering throughout my life. I was still a child when I stood on the church stage for the first time, in front of the congregation, and recited the words to the Twenty-third Psalm.

And so I always know that I am at one with all of God's creatures: His dogs and cats, His sons and daughters. In the deepest part of my being, I know for certain that I am never alone.

Yea, though I walk through the valley
of the shadow of death,
I will fear no evil; for Thou art with me;
Thy rod and Thy staff they comfort me

As I walk through the shadows of my past, as my mind jumps from one moment to the next, I see that the joys of my childhood far out-weighed the difficulties. I had enthusiasm, and I had hopes, goals, and aspirations that were mostly supported and nurtured.

Maybe at that moment, God gave my life this grace. My faith and truth are so deep, they're my private secret. I know why so many wonderful things have happened in my life, like my relationship with my inner voice, and I am so thankful.

69

Under the African Skies

A privacy
appears on the surface
ordinary and common
bearer of light
stand on the mountain
free in my thinking

The Blues
consider me a colored girl
me
head full of stars
heart full

Schools in America don't teach a lot about the black experience in the United States. There was never enough information about Africa. We touched on our history but not enough as to how blacks contributed to life in America. It was as if we weren't here at all.

The textbooks had an insulting and misleading name for Africa: They called it the "Dark Continent." Today, I understand why, but to a child, that sounded scary. It seemed as if black people lived in a sunless, forbidding place.

As for slavery, my teachers only talked briefly about plantations (they made it sound romantic as in *Gone With the Wind*), Abraham

Lincoln, and the War Between the States. To find the few black history books in the public schools you had to search, and teachers never really told their classes the real details about how black people lived in America. I think today it's better, but there should be more.

I made sure my children went to schools that would provide them with good educations and expose them to many different experiences. Their world has been a mixture of all the races. I've created an environment in which they are able to be treated as human beings and always know that their heritage is a wonderful part of their lives.

I want them to hear something in school and then come home and be able to interact with all the people who are around them and love them. Then, when they take a stand on an issue, they will have all the information. They can come out strong and make a statement about being a woman or about abortion or whatever.

72

I have done as best as I know how for my children. If I have missed anything, then it is just because I did not know any better. I have given them as much as I can. I like to think of what I've done as life lessons. And part of these life lessons was our vacation in Africa.

We went to Africa in 1986 expecting to find out more about who I was and to see where a great part of my heritage came from. It was a powerful experience, even though I didn't really find what I was looking for.

I went to the majestically beautiful country of Kenya with my daughters and visited friends of my husband. I had traveled there before, but this was a special time for me and my girls. The land, the animals were so lovely and compelling. We toured the land by jeep and by helicopter, taking pictures as we soared over the terrain. Sometimes, especially from above, the earth looked as though it had ringworms because of all the dry patches. Other parts were emerald with a tangle of jungle. And there were dry and flat areas with a golden, sandy color. We sat outside at night with bats flying all over the place.

While I was with the Samburu tribe, I had a powerful and moving experience. I walked among the girls who were all caked in red mud and dressed in a rainbow of beads, rows and rows of beads crawling up their necks. I was singled out because of my skin color, and while the others in our party watched, they did their traditional colored paintings on my body and face. I was taken in, lost in the dance they danced around me, as they took the red mud paint from their skin and put it on my face. I wasn't sure how they felt about me, but I was in a magical trance. Their beads seemed to undulate as they circled me, touching my face, giggling. I walked away, my feet not touching the ground, feeling blessed and close, with a sense of knowing.

I wanted to have this connection to my black heritage. Going to Africa was like stepping back into history. I actually made two trips to Africa, as I felt that I could not make a deep enough connection in only one trip. We flew to Nairobi and stepped into a vibrant land filled with black people. And once we took off for the bush, I experienced the "real" land: animals running free, scampering over their ravishing domain. We lived in tents, ate outside under the African skies, and every night made a blazing fire to protect us from the dangerous animals.

73

It was a rich land, made richer by what we didn't have, rather than by what we had. There were no telephones or televisions to distract us. Instead, we had elephants and giraffes and other glories of the wild. We went to a village one day and the people there looked at my daughters and me as if we were exotic animals in a zoo. I had a video camera, which they didn't seem to object to very much because the flash of still cameras is what they find disturbing and frightening. We went inside their homes and saw where they sleep. They sleep on the ground with little headrests to keep the bugs out of their hair. I bought a few of these headrests and a couple of chairs from them, which have become a part of my African art collection. I have an incredible African collection. Accumulating such a treasury is derived from a love for beauty. And African art and artifacts are truly lovely. I think back to the 1970s when wearing dashikis was fashionable. There were so many shawls and fabrics and other materials that were absolutely fabulous.

In Kenya, we met many Masai families and learned how they exist from day to day. The cow, we found out, is very sacred to them. They actually drink the cow's blood, mixed with a little milk. They cut a vein on the cow's neck and allow the blood to trickle into a cup made from a gourd or seed. Then they milk the cow and blend the two liquids. The drink, they say, is important for strength.

Much of the trip was a beautiful adventure, but there was one occasion that caused alarm. One day, the men in our group went off to find elephants and left the women, the cooks, and one or two others behind at the camp. Suddenly, a group of Africans invaded the camps. They wore city clothes and had a certain menace to them. I was frightened; we all were frightened. Apparently, they wanted our jewelry and watches. I was told to stay in the tent, but this was Diana they were talking to—a Detroit girl who had learned not to back down. So I took it upon myself to come out and let them see me because I really thought that if they saw me, a black woman, they wouldn't loot or hurt anyone. I didn't think they would know who Diana Ross was, so I said I was an "American singer." Surprisingly, they seemed to know my name. In fact, one of the guys had a tape recorder and was playing a Luther Vandross song! So they just inspected us, walked through our tents, and left us alone. It was a strange and scary experience for me. I had come to Africa to be with my friends and also to connect to my heritage, only to feel the same way I would feel if a mugger approached me in New York. I desperately wanted to have this connection.

There's so much all of us, black and white, can learn from Africa. After all, when Europe was in its Stone Age, African communities were working with iron. The first slaves who were uprooted from their African countries and brought to America in 1619 came from highly organized societies in which economic activity flourished and education was important. African cultures were complex and developed centuries ago—just look at the great empires of Songhay, Ghana, and Melle.

I learned so much while I was there. I met individuals from the Rendille and the Turkana tribes. At Lake Beringo, I met the Pakot tribe. I found out about the University of Sankore near the river Niger where Africans in the fifteenth century studied law and geography and medicine. This was real. And it gave me a great sense of pride. I even considered finding a farm in Africa. And yes, it was clear that family was very, very important to Africans.

Sometimes at night during my travels, I would stand alone outside the tent and think about what life was like so long ago and where I came from.

I stood on golden soil under a sapphire sky that could have sheltered one of my ancestors and breathed the African air. So many different scents and spices, all natural, pungent, and sweet. Although I was a stranger in a strange land, I felt a sense of belonging, of being a part of something much greater than I had ever known. Kenya made me feel so peaceful, so calm. I closed my eyes and inhaled this marvelous continent, and memories of things I never experienced awakened something in me. It made me cry, and I wept for those who had gone before me, tears for myself, for my children. My children, my precious babies. They are growing up in a very difficult period, a time filled with tension and hostility between the races.

I grew up in the midst of great change. During the 1960s and '70s, people were trying to cure all the pain in the world. Blacks were trying to get past all the nonsense of bigotry—we really thought that was in the past. I thought that the sixties were a pulling-together. A time of healing. How and why we started to back up is beyond me, but I'm sure poverty and economics play a big part.

Today, my areas of concern have to do with children. Many people talk about ecology, but I want to talk about America's children—all of America's children, not only black children.

In the sixties, the issue was clear, and it was made even more illuminating by Dr. Martin Luther King. In August 1963, he delivered his magnificent "I Have a Dream" speech before the Lincoln Memorial. His words still fill my heart:

> *I say to you today, my friends, that in spite of the difficulties and frustrations of the moment, I still have a dream. It is a dream deeply rooted in the American dream. I have a dream that one day this nation will rise up and live out the true meaning of its creed:*
>
> *"We hold these truths to be self-evident; that all men are created equal."*

When Dr. King was assassinated, I thought that someone had just pulled the ground from under my feet. I was in New York watching it all on television, and I, like people throughout the world, was shocked. I just couldn't believe what was happening. I remember seeing him lying there, hoping he would be all right but knowing deep in my heart that he would not be. It was as if the whole world was falling apart.

The Supremes had been scheduled to give a performance at the Copacabana in New York City on the day that Dr. King died. That show was canceled. The next night, we appeared on *The Tonight Show* and sang our version of "Somewhere," incorporating lines from Dr. King's "I Have a Dream" speech. We found a way of working his breathtaking prose into Leonard Bernstein's song about a place where people can live without prejudice:

When we let freedom ring, when we let it ring from every village and every hamlet, from every state and every city, we will be able to speed up that day when all God's children, black men and white men, Jews and Gentiles, Protestants and Catholics, will be able to join hands and sing in the words of the old Negro spiritual, "Free at last! Free at last! Thank God Almighty, we are free at last."

In a strange way, I think something did end there. He was the last of our heroes who could make it happen and who were willing to put their lives on the line and try to make changes for the betterment of humanity.

I was in a deep depression for a long time after he died. He had touched me in a profound way. I felt a sense of hopelessness. It was not just a life that had gone, but something else had left.

I felt the pain for Coretta, and I loved her beauty and how regally she held herself. I had marveled at how Jackie Kennedy had conducted herself, too. And I wondered about myself: Would I have been able to be as strong, to stand as tall as these women had? I thought about that as I sat at the funeral and later at Dr. King's burial. I saw Coretta quite a few times after that. She is a wonderful woman, and I know she tried to carry on.

But Dr. King was really the leader. He *was* the movement. I was just hoping that someone else would be able to move into the forefront and become the leader, but no one ever did. And that's fine because we don't always have to have leaders. Sometimes we need to come together to support each other and strive as individuals to achieve better relationships between people. Together we stand, divided we fall. And we should never forget where we came from.

I think a lot about all the people who came before me—not just my parents and grandparents but their parents and grandparents and all the other black and brown people who gave their lives so that those of us who came later would be free. So many people, so many sacrifices. People I never knew gave me the freedom of choice and freedom of opportunity that have allowed me to become who I am today. And there were those I was fortunate to have known, such as Martin Luther King, if only briefly, like a flicker in time.

I have tried to open up opportunities for blacks, for women, for minorities. Every time I go into a project, my first thought is about hiring as many minorities as are capable of doing the work. Even on tours—when we're looking for promoters, we look for a black person or a minority promoter who otherwise might not get the opportunity to work. I open windows of opportunity and go for the best.

I guess wanting the best and striving for perfection goes back to my parents, who taught us never to settle for anything less that what we wanted, deserved, or needed. My mother gave me a tremendous amount of common sense and taught us to be the best we could be at whatever we chose to follow and to be true to ourselves. I knew from an early age that regardless of what I wanted to do, what I went after in life, my journey would be harder than others'. That's because black people have to strive harder. Yes, at times it's been difficult, but good things can come from adversity.

When I look back, it seems that all the grief that had to be in my life eventually left me. And when the pain was over, I was stronger than before. A part of me comes from our cruel past, from slavery, from the days of lynchings and segregation. I will never take any freedom for granted. I will never take my blackness for granted. I will never take my humanity for granted.

I certainly had more opportunities than my grandparents or their grandparents. But as a black woman in the entertainment business, I know all too well about discrimination and injustice.

My life and career were made easier by others who suffered indignities and stood up to certain abuses. I'm talking about such women as the great contralto Marian Anderson, the gracious Lena Horne, the inspirational Ethel Waters, the fragile and vulnerable Dorothy Dandridge, the brave and exotic Josephine Baker, and scores of others: Billie, Bessie, Sarah, and Ella.

There are scars, and there are also small victories. Still, I know that as a black woman, I remain in bondage. I know that all black people do, in spite of the tremendous advances we have made over the century. That's because the one thing none of us has been able to destroy completely is hate. If God gave me one job in life, it is to help create a world in which we are all just people.

My love and appreciation of humanity and life extends to all people. There are little parts of me that have come from many other cultures and heritages because, as Americans, we are all very mixed. We are all beautiful—black, white, brown, yellow, red. I see the joy on people's faces, the inner spirit, the richness of heritage and history. These realities fill my heart, and I want to jump up and sing "Hallelujah."

To me, we are all one part of the human race. I've raised my children to believe in themselves, to respect and appreciate each human being.

My mother gave me those special values, and I know my children have the strength of character to pass those same virtues on to their children. I want my children to know where they came from. A sense of history gives us a sense of self.

However, there is so much in the world I want all my children to see—a quality I want them to appreciate in the human race. I want them to realize the possibilities that exist in the world for all of us truly to live as one.

I have been to just about every corner of the world, and I have met people from as many different backgrounds and cultures as there can possibly be. When I am up there on stage singing and I see the faces in the audience and touch their hands—and I hope their hearts—I realize more than ever that we're all just people.

Down and Dirty

A s a child, my parents did not discuss anything racial. Our world was small then, living on St. Antoine Street. I do not remember traveling too far out of that circle to see what the rest of the world was like. My world was two blocks long. If my parents confronted a lot of racism in their lives, I did not know it at that time. I was protected. Or maybe they were just too busy raising six children.

One incident was the talk of the town. That was the brutal murder of Emmett Till. I read about him in *Jet* magazine. We kids even passed the magazine around, staring at the picture of Emmett's body, seeing the chilling horror of what had happened to a fourteen-year-old boy in the South. I was very taken by that story.

Even today, I think about it and shudder...

Emmett Till was a black teenager from Chicago who went to Money, Mississippi, to visit relatives. One day, he supposedly whistled at the wife of a white shopkeeper. His body, mutilated and filled with bullet holes, was pulled from the Tallahatchie River on August 31, 1955. The two white men accused of murdering him later were acquitted by an all-white, all-male jury.

I will never forget Emmett Till. And it is good to know that others also will not allow his memory to languish. Part of a Chicago street was renamed for Emmett by Mayor Richard Daley in 1991 "as a visible reminder of the tragic consequences of racism and hatred." His name also is carved on the Civil Rights Memorial in Montgomery, Alabama,

OPPOSITE PAGE:
We should never forget where we come from.
If I had my way, there would be no prejudice.

right there with Martin Luther King and others who lost their lives for freedom and justice. In her play *Dreaming Emmett,* Toni Morrison gave the whole period a dreadful and compelling intimacy, just like the pictures in *Jet* magazine.

Emmett Till was a little close to the skin. It made me very frightened. I did not think things like that would ever happen in the North; I certainly hoped they wouldn't. I thought we were lucky we did not have to live in the South.

During a few summers when we were young, my parents would send us to visit relatives in Bessemer, Alabama. There is little I recall about those trips in the 1950s, little I can remember about the South. A part of me seems to have forgotten those early experiences with segregation. I dimly recall seeing signs on water fountains, in waiting rooms, and at movie theaters: WHITE, COLORED. In those days—in the South especially—whites called black people "colored." We called ourselves "Negroes." It's funny how words and names change. In the 1950s, we didn't dare call ourselves "black." And then, once we got used to being called "black," we changed to "African-American."

Those trips south were my first experiences with bigotry. As dim as my recollections are about that time, my brother Fred and my sisters, Rita and Bobbi, have vivid memories of those trips. We talked about Bessemer while I was preparing this book. Fred, Rita, and Bobbi helped fill in the spaces my mind had blanked out over the years.

There were so many indignities black people endured; everything was separate and unequal. When we took the Greyhound bus from Detroit to Bessemer, we had to change our seats in Cincinnati, Ohio, and move to the back of the bus. When we stopped to use rest rooms, we were forced to use the horrible and smelly areas marked "colored" and drink from the rusty and dirty water fountains reserved for black people. Facilities for whites were generally clean and newer than those set aside for us.

Segregation did not stop in the 1950s but continued well into the sixties and, in some areas, even the seventies. I remember flying down to Alabama once after I had first started singing. When I arrived at the airport, I got off the plane and walked into the terminal, just as I did when I was at any other airport. But my Aunt Willie was waiting for me in a different part of the terminal. Apparently, I had walked into the "white" section. I remember a white person walking up to me, trying to be polite and nice, saying, "We think you are in the wrong place."

Yes. I was in the wrong place. It was a place I did not enjoy visiting. I truly did not like going down there.

One summer we were forced to remain in Bessemer for a year because Mama was sick with tuberculosis and in the hospital. I was about eight years old at the time, and none of us knew Mama was sick. In fact, it wasn't until we were young adults that we found out she had TB. At the time, we didn't know we would be going to school in the South until we were safely tucked away at Aunt Willie's, stuck in the South with Uncle Daniel and segregation.

I always wondered why no one ever questioned the system at the time. Everyone just did it or accepted things because that's the way it was and they did not want any trouble.

In the North, we accepted a certain way of life, but we did not think of it as segregation. Still, I lived in an all-black neighborhood, and until I went to junior high school, I had attended all-black grade schools.

Our thought processes and acceptance of a segregated society began to change with people like Rosa Parks. Rosa, a black woman, sat up front and refused to move to the back of a bus in Montgomery, Alabama. This was the same period in which Martin Luther King helped forge the civil rights movement. He was trying to put an end to an unjust, inhuman, and irrational system.

Still, the violence and hate did not stop. To this day, we all believe that my cousin Virginia Ruth was murdered by the Ku Klux Klan. We thought she had been in a car accident, but there were no skid marks, no marks on the car—just her body at the side of the road.

Virginia Ruth was the cousin we stayed with when we visited Aunt Willie in Bessemer. And it was Virginia Ruth who was supposed to grow up to be a singer, not me. They called her the "Girl with the Golden Voice" because she could sing so beautifully. She planned to become a professional singer, and she sang in church. At the time of her death, she had been teaching at Spelman College in Atlanta, driving back and forth from Bessemer to Atlanta. Another promising young black life had been snuffed out.

Years later, my brother T-Boy went south and almost got killed. He had gone to a little store and bought a bag of chips. He stood there, opened up the bag, and plopped down a ten- or twenty-dollar bill on the counter. The shopkeeper said he didn't have change for a twenty so he'd just keep the whole thing. Well, T-Boy yelled, "Give me back my money. I want my money." Someone came from the back of the store with a knife to chase him out, and then the police arrived. A policeman pulled out his gun, and T-Boy was very nearly killed as a shot grazed his ear. I lived in California at the time and had to try and get him out of a difficult situation.

This was in the 1960s. It's hard to believe, but we all seem to forget that our nation's capital was segregated in the sixties as it still is today, in many areas. At that time, if you were black and accustomed to a certain amount of mobility in the North, you didn't want to face the restrictions of the South.

I remember going there once while on tour with the Supremes. My manager, Shelly Berger, and I went into a little pizza shop to pick up something to eat. He walked over to the counter to order the pizza, and I went to the jukebox to check out the music. There were a lot of people there, but I did not know if they were black, white, or whatever. After a while, I looked up and saw a guy talking to Shelly and suddenly leading him outside. He told Shelly that if he did not get me out of there, they were going to do something bad to him. Shelly came back in and told me what had happened and said we had to leave. That's when I got real strappy. I huffed and puffed myself up to my full height and started thrashing about, screaming, "Leave? What do you mean I've got to leave?" And it did not occur to me that I was in real danger, as was Shelly. Those guys were ready to rip us apart.

We were all very upset by that act of discrimination and near violence. There was tremendous disbelief that something like that could happen. We had to perform the same night to a very mixed audience, and it was a wonderful, wonderful show with whites and blacks all having a good time together.

What happened did not make me hate a whole race of people, but once again I realized that there are some terrible people in the world. After that, when the Supremes toured in the South, we knew we had to be careful about where we went and what we did, and it probably did make the image of Emmett Till surface once again in my mind.

Did these incidents have an influence on my life? I'm sure they did, but they did not change my love and respect for humanity and did not make me judge the white friends and associates I had. I found that there are wonderful, decent people and mean, bad people in both the black and white worlds.

Loyalty, commitment, honor. These are simple, yet complex things. But all three are important creeds in my life. Simply put, it's the Golden Rule: Do unto others as you would have them do unto you.

Reflections Of...

The Primettes

M y story has often been referred to as classic "rags to riches," but in truth, that description doesn't fit me at all. For starters, the Rosses were never raggedy. We may not have had a lot of money, and every moment was not great, but I was brought up to have ideals, to believe that anything was possible and that hard work was a part of that. With these ideals, so many things just clicked in a beautiful harmony. I feel very fortunate to have gotten to where I am from where I was.

I don't think that I ever thought, "You can't get anywhere from here." Those words never really formed in my mind because there was no place that I knew I wanted to go. Until I was about ten years old, I didn't know there was a world out there to explore. A wondrous world. I simply took life as it came and took advantage of each opportunity that presented itself. And I never accepted the idea that I couldn't achieve something that I wanted. I was taught that I could.

OPPOSITE PAGE:
We loved to sing more than anything.
We used to get together and rehearse
as often as we could, but had no idea
how to get to the next step.

OVERLEAF:
When you want something bad enough,
somehow it happens. Singing opened up a
world filled with wonder and possibilities.

My life could have taken so many different turns. I could easily have become tough; some of the neighborhood bullies were my friends. I used to watch the prostitutes who walked the streets nearby. Although I admired their flashy clothes, I could feel the sadness in their hearts. I knew that I had something different ahead of me. I had no idea what it was, I just lived my life and kept moving.

I can't remember when I actually began singing; I think I always sang. I must have come out of the womb that way. I used to trail after my mother when she did her household chores, the walls of our apartment swelling with music: jazz, blues, Etta James. To me, Etta was the One, my original inspiration. The shock of hearing a voice so powerful and so deep made me marvel that one young woman could claim such power and passion! When I was still a very small child, I remember sneaking off by myself and entering into my own little world of entertainment. I would stand up in front of the mirror in a trance, watching my lips move and my body sway as I sang along with an Etta record like "Dance with Me, Henry," performing for a wildly cheering, imaginary audience. At those times, I felt alive and in my element. I didn't know that my destiny would be a life on the stage singing, but I always wanted the best out of life.

After our first home on St. Antoine, we moved to 635 Belmont. It was there that I met my handsome neighbor William Robinson, better known to the world as Smokey. While still in my early teens, I had a girlfriend named Sharon Burstyn, who was Smokey Robinson's niece. They lived right down the street from me. When I slept over at her house, she and I would spend hours sitting on the basement steps, watching her uncle rehearse with his group called the Miracles. One day when I was at a friend's house, we turned on the radio and I heard a familiar sound:

Walked all day 'til my feet were tired.
Got a job.

One of Smokey's records, "Got a Job," had actually gotten radio play. It was his first release and his first hit. I was thrilled. I rushed home, crashed through the front door, and yelled, "Mama, Smokey's made a record, and they're playing it on the radio! He did it!" I knew that if he could do it, I could do it, too. It made me feel like nothing was impossible. At the time, I had no far-reaching dreams to become a celebrity or a movie star. I just wanted to make a record. I wanted to sing. It became a reality to me that afternoon, when I heard that Smokey and the Miracles record on the radio, that someone could actually record a song and have a hit and that thousands of people would hear it.

I was fourteen when we moved from 635 Belmont to the Brewster housing projects in Detroit. In high school, I did the regular things that teenage girls do. I swam, and I played baseball. I was a tomboyish type, with rolled-up bangs in front and either a ponytail in the back or two pigtails sticking out on the sides. I loved to dance, so I also took tap dance and majorette classes at Brewster Center, a fantastic recreation place.

In the Brewster projects, on those hot and sultry Detroit nights, everybody gathered at the corner or sat on the three little steps in the doorways of their apartments. I used to have to be in the house by the time the streetlights came on, but if my parents made me come in early, I would yell out my windows to my friends who were located within earshot, or, sometimes, I would sneak out. Once I got caught. When Mama came looking for me, she found me at a dance in the dark basement of a friend's house. I was so embarrassed in front of the other kids when she made me leave. At the same time she reached for me, I was pulling away and her hand accidentally connected with my nose. Suddenly, blood came pouring out of my nose. I knew she hadn't done it on purpose, but I just let the blood run down my face and all over my shirt. Mama felt so bad, so terribly guilty, she forgot to be mad at me. I sure was a mischievous little devil.

In the daytime of the summer months, we played a lot of baseball, and then somebody would open up a fire hydrant. We'd have great street showers, shrieking with joy and running in and out of the flying water. There was always music playing, and I loved to sing around the neighborhood, everybody did. I had a boyfriend named Tommy Rodgers, who lived just across the street, and he used to walk me to school. Tommy was a really good singer and we sang a lot together, so word got around that I had a good voice. That was how I first made friends after we moved to the projects, by singing.

It was there in the Detroit Brewster projects that I met Mary Wilson and Florence Ballard. I came from a very religious family. My mother's father was a Baptist minister, and she and her sisters had all been raised to be gospel singers. Although Mary and I went to the same church, she and Florence went to Northeastern High, while I went to Cass Tech. Because of the community spirit in the neighborhood, we managed to get together to sing. The three of us hit it off. When we first started singing together, we did it on a casual basis. As people, we couldn't have been more different, but our voices made an interesting blend and so did our personalities.

Florence was tall, proud, and beautiful, with fair skin and fine hair. She was absolutely regal, and the strength in her voice matched her carriage. She was capable of such high volume that, with the proper training, maybe she could have sung opera if she had had the money or the knowledge to pursue that kind of a career. The truth is that some of the early love songs like "Baby Love" and "Where Did Our Love Go" were too petite for her and just didn't match the depth of her voice. The record business was looking for something that sounded like the Chantels or the Shirelles. Mary Wilson proved to be a buffer. Despite the fact that Mary mostly sang the lower tones, she had a beautiful harmony voice with a great deal of warmth to it. She fit so well with Florence and me; she carried the exact sound just between the two of us that blended all our voices together, the sound that made up the perfect harmony so that we were like one voice. And Mary had charisma onstage. She was the sexy one; she loved to wiggle her hips, bat her eyes at the men in the front row, and give off a "come and get me" attitude. Florence was much more standoffish; her regalness would never allow her to demonstrate that kind of raw energy. She had a very different way of being.

I was more aligned with Florence in that way. Although we had a childlike sex appeal, I never chose to express it blatantly. I didn't wiggle my hips or bat my eyes. I wasn't interested in manipulating men by bumping or grinding. I was always interested in elegance and the music, and I was singing for the pure enjoyment of it. My gift was being able, simply and honestly, to express the emotions of a song. For that reason, my voice worked best as lead singer on the kind of material we used and I was able to balance the other two, becoming a blend of Mary's sexual energy and Florence's regal attitude. The three of us together made an unbeatable combination.

I must have been no more than fourteen or fifteen when we first started singing together because I remember that I was still walking to school every day. It was the spring of '59 and I was just finishing the ninth grade. At that time, Betty McGlowan was also a part of the group. She didn't live in the projects; she lived over on the west side of town. She was a beautiful girl, tall, very thin, and dark-skinned. A good singer. When she left us to get married, she and I lost touch.

We loved to sing more than anything, and we used to get together and rehearse as often as we could, with no idea how to get to the next step. When you want something bad enough, somehow it happens. Florence, who was from a very big family, had a beautiful older sister. I think she was dating a manager named Milton Jenkins. He dressed really slick and cruised around in a big red Cadillac convertible. It was Milton Jenkins who really got us started when he brought around this group of guys from Alabama to meet us girls.

Milton Jenkins thought that our group and Cal, Eddie, and Paul, who called themselves the Primes and were trying to make an act for themselves, might be a good match to sing together. Although we never performed with them until much later on when we were the Supremes and they were the Temptations, we used to rehearse with them after school.

Using the name the Primettes, we became a sister group to these guys, and Milton Jenkins started managing us, too. After Betty left, we were only three, but we still felt that we needed a fourth, so we took on Barbara Martin. The four of us sang and rehearsed together for the next few years. So you see, changes within the group had already begun happening before we ever walked in the door of Motown for that first audition.

Singing became my life. I lived, ate, drank, and breathed it. It was all that I cared about. I had a dream, and I was completely determined to make it real. Nothing could deter me or discourage me for very long. My only obstacle was Daddy. Two of the guys from the Primes, Cal and

Eddie, tried to intervene one day when they came over to ask my mother if I could please sing with them. Mama put up a fuss at first, but she understood my obsession and my determination. If I promised to get my schoolwork done, she would give her permission. But Daddy was a different story. He was a practical man, a solemn man, and he was very much opposed to my taking singing seriously. He was certain that singing would distract me from my schoolwork. He wanted me to go to college and get a good education so that I would be well equipped to take care of myself in a highly competitive world, one in which education would be the single most important element. I was happy that he wanted me to be somebody special, but I was fourteen years old. I had not suffered the trials of life that he had undergone, and I had my own dreams. It was very difficult to get his permission to be a Primette. I finally managed, but in those days it was a struggle with him each step of the way.

The Primettes continued to rehearse, and soon, when we felt ready, we began to perform at neighborhood parties. We loved performing, and the harder we worked, the hotter our act became. Sometimes when we were hired to perform at a large event, we were announced on the radio: "The Primettes will be performing at such and such a place at such and such a time." The mere mention of our names brought us a great deal of pride and excitement. We may have been young, but we were seriously working toward our goal. We were determined to cut a record. Music, even at this stage in my development, was already giving my life the magic and meaning I so desperately wanted. I knew that with my music, I had something of my own and it would last me a lifetime if I so desired. Singing was always a gift, whether it was rehearsing, performing, or just playing around with the other kids in the neighborhood. It brought me pleasure and self-confidence, especially when I saw that I could make people smile and move their bodies. Being an inspiration to the people around me was one of my greatest joys, and it still is.

Florence, Mary, Barbara, and I had been singing together for a couple of years when I finally decided to ask Smokey Robinson if he could get us an audition with Berry Gordy at Motown. Berry Gordy was managing Smokey and the Miracles, they had a big hit song, and they were already a big deal. We felt lucky to know somebody who had an in to Berry Gordy and Motown. We wanted to be given a chance; we just needed an audition, and then we would be well on our way. Perhaps this kind of innocence, blind determination, and naiveté were my greatest strengths. Failure was impossible because I made no space within to consider anything negative; I could only visualize success.

Smokey and I were good friends. We had gotten to know each other when I lived on Belmont, so I felt that I could call him to hear us sing. My plan was that he would like us and get us the audition that we wanted. One day, the girls and I were all together, driving in a car, when we spotted a tall, skinny-looking guy walking down the street with a big guitar on his back.

"Stop the car!" I said. We all watched him for a few minutes, and we all sensed a kind of sweetness emitting from him. That was what made me feel safe enough to talk to him. For some reason, he didn't feel like a stranger, and I just knew that he would be great.

"That's our guitar player. I just know that's him," I told the girls. Now I needed to drum up the courage to talk to him.

"But what are you going to say to him? He doesn't know us. Why would he want to play for us?" somebody asked.

"We'll just ask him," I said. "We'll just ask him to play for us, cuz we're good." So I opened up the window and yelled out, "Hey, you. We're singers. You wanna play for us? You want to play guitar for us?" He must have thought we were crazy, but he smiled and we got his telephone number. His name was Marvin Tarplin, and it turned out that he was a great guitar player and a wonderful person. That's how it happened. It seems that in those days there was a strange kind of magic flowing through the air, arranging things and creating a synergy, making everything happen as if it had been preplanned. Maybe it was a lack of resistance, an innocence of youth that just trusts the process as it unfolds.

I don't know what Marvin was doing before our encounter on the street, but we started rehearsing with him right away and it worked out beautifully. He played really well, and he knew all the current songs. When we felt we were ready, I called Smokey.

"Smokey, I have a group. Would you please listen to us?" I asked him.

95

To my delight he agreed. It wasn't really an audition. Smokey was still young, and he wasn't an executive at Motown yet. But we knew that if he liked us, he had the power to set something up for us. We went to one of Smokey's choir rehearsals and sang our hearts out. I'll always remember that evening; it was the night Smokey stole Marvin, our guitar player. He took him on the road, but he also set up the audition for us. A loss and a gain. I think Marvin still plays with him.

Rats, roaches, guts, and love. That was how Berry Gordy described Motown in the early days. These words may have confused people who took him literally. He was talking about the nitty-gritty of life then, of the elements that went into making a record company happen in a big way. Creating Motown and making it a success was a massive undertaking, a bold dream, a courageous vision. And Berry Gordy had what it took to do it.

Smokey accompanied us to Motown for our audition, to the building we called Hitsville, USA. We were so nervous we hardly knew what to do with ourselves. There were so many people trying to get record deals at Motown, and we were young high school girls from the projects, trying to be recording artists. But what we lacked in experience, we made up in enthusiasm.

Hitsville is still there to this day. I can remember the way it was in vivid detail. It was so simple, just a strange little square room. A drum set stood in the far right-hand corner beside a staircase that led downward into another room below. Microphones were set up all over the room, and the engineers used to move them around to create different sounds.

We stood up there in a straight line in front of some Motown representatives to do our audition, our nerves on edge, our emotions highly amplified. They were all strangers to us. Smokey wasn't in the room; he was waiting outside. We sang a few songs a cappella that we had painstakingly prepared for this day. The tension was high; we knew this was a pivotal moment for us. We did our very best songs. I remember Florence doing the lead on one of our favorite Ray Charles songs, I think it was "Night Time Is the Right Time," and I did the high voice. That was our third song. Then, in the middle of the last one, "There Goes My Baby," a song in which I sang lead, Berry Gordy himself came walking into the room. We had never met him before, we had only heard about him, but we instantly knew who he was. The man had a presence. You could feel the energy shift and crackle as the others reacted to their boss entering the room. He was obviously on his way to somewhere else, but he paused momentarily to listen to us. Without as much as a glance at each other, we knew we were being watched and we knew who was watching us, so we performed for him. Our movements got bigger, and our voices became more expressive. He stood there until we finished the song and he said, "Sing that song over again, 'There Goes My Baby.'" So we did. "Very nice, girls. Very nice." That was all he said, and then he swiftly left the room.

I think we did a great job in our first audition. Our energies were already connected and very good together. I thought so at the time, and I was anxious to hear what Mr. Gordy would have to say to us. Of course we wanted to get signed right then and there. We waited a little while for him to talk to us—it felt like forever. I remember the extreme anxiety of sitting in that room, so afraid, because I knew that Berry Gordy was the man who could make or break us. When he finally came back, he was somewhat encouraging. He liked us, he liked our sound, but he insisted that we were too young for a contract.

"Go and finish school, work on your music, and then come back and audition again."

We were heartbroken. We were impetuous teenagers, impatient and headstrong. I wanted to convince the head of Motown that we were ready right now, that we were already good enough, that we could easily handle both school and a recording deal, but I said nothing. It was pretty obvious from just being with him that his mind was made up and that once Berry Gordy made up his mind, nobody went against him. We left very discouraged but in no way broken-down. In fact, I think we were more determined than ever. Berry Gordy was not the only one who knew what he wanted. I have never been able to take no for an answer, and he had definitely not seen the last of me. In fact, it was quite clear to me that the relationship had only just begun.

Buttered Popcorn

A lthough we did our first record on the Lupine label before we met Berry Gordy, we had definitely set our sights on Motown. It was in 1959, and we were still the Primettes. We had tried writing our own song. It was called "Tears of Sorrow," and it went something like this:

> *Tears of sorrow, cry for tomorrow,*
> *I'll just have to cry again, so why wait 'til then?*
> *All my happiness, gone, and I guess*
> *I'll just have to cry again, so why wait 'til then?*

I can still hear that song repeating in my head. It's funny how the mind holds on to certain words.

During the entire year of 1960, on just about any given afternoon, if somebody asked my mother where I was, the answer would almost always be the same: "She's at Motown." In the early part of 1960, after the famous audition in which Berry refused us a contract, the other girls and I decided that if Motown was where we wanted to be, why waste time anywhere else? We could hardly wait for school to get out so we could ride the bus to that building every day. Everybody at Motown got used to seeing us; we quickly became permanent fixtures there. At first we just hung around, trying every kind of persuasion we could muster to get them to give us a contract. We met all the recording artists, and

OPPOSITE PAGE:
Motown became the "hit factory."

very soon, although we hadn't yet gotten the contract we so wanted, we did manage to sing backup for some of the established groups. We were paid next to nothing, but money meant very little to us then. It was all valuable experience, and in those days we were thrilled to be doing anything there at all. Berry was in and out all the time, and we got to make contact with him. Everybody wanted his attention, and we loved being able to see him and stay somewhat in his focus. So we were busy all the time, getting our homework done as well and as fast as we could, rehearsing, and performing at parties as the Primettes and doing background singing for Motown at Hitsville.

In the summer of 1960, the Primettes traveled across the river from Detroit to Windsor, Ontario. We had decided to compete in an amateur talent contest, and we were very excited. It was a fulfillment of a part of our dream. We were not only traveling for the first time, we were doing it as performers. Needless to say, we were very nervous. We were merely teenagers, and this contest, which drew on talent from both Detroit and Canada, had attracted an audience of thousands. After performing mostly at record hops and community events, this felt like the big time.

As we walked out onto the stage, my heart sped up and a shot of adrenaline rushed up my spine. This was what I loved and what I wanted to do. All eyes were on us as we sang our standard songs, "Night Time Is the Right Time" and "There Goes My Baby." We were revved up, we had rehearsed hard for this, and the audience cheered and screamed when we were finished. We won the contest, but, more important, I had my first taste of the delicious feelings that come with creating a rapport with so many people at the same time and the sense of being appreciated and rewarded for a job well done. We all left elated, and we wanted more of it.

In order to maintain the support of my parents, I had to be very careful at home, making sure I got my schoolwork done. Florence had a similar agreement with her parents, but she wasn't as conscientious as I was. Her parents, like mine, although they wanted her to sing, were extremely concerned because she wasn't doing well at school right from the beginning. She was from a big family; she had eleven brothers and sisters. Her parents wanted her to be successful in her life. They were so afraid she'd drop out of school, and then she would have no solid base and no way to provide for her future. In fact, that's exactly what did happen to some of her siblings. Many times Mary and I went to her house to meet with her parents to try to persuade them to let her sing with us. We promised them we would make sure that she studied and did her homework. Finally, they said yes. We had gotten rid of the immediate obstacles.

Florence was not easy. She had a strong personality, just like her voice. Everything about her was big. When she was happy, it was contagious. Everybody was happy. When she was unhappy, everybody around her felt miserable. She was terribly moody, constantly up and down. And she was hard to figure out; we could never really understand what drove her moods. We never knew if we had done something to offend her and she wouldn't tell us. So she'd be in some dark mood, and then, miraculously and suddenly, it was over. Of course we were always 101 relieved when she resurfaced, but we were also frustrated because we were none the wiser about what had caused the emotional roller-coaster. She was secretive about her feelings, so she was the one everybody tried to appease. You know how the old adage goes: The squeaky wheel gets the grease. When Florence squeaked, it was just like being with the Tinman from *The Wizard of Oz*. We ran over with the oil can and usually managed to get her working again, but we never knew exactly where to oil her or why she was squeaking. Maybe she didn't know herself. With Florence, there always seemed to be a problem; nothing was ever right no matter how hard we tried to please her. It was difficult. Mary and I both cared for her, and we wanted her to be happy. I wanted everyone to be happy.

Before Florence died, on February 22, 1976, I honestly did not know that she was as sick as she was or that she was anywhere close to death. The fact that she died young feels like a waste. It didn't have to happen. She was a great success and a winner. She had already grabbed the brass ring, but she threw it away. I don't know why this happens in life, and I certainly don't know why it happened to Florence. I never understood her. Florence's life was always shrouded in mystery for me. I don't think she ever wanted to be a singer as much as her family wanted it for her and ultimately for themselves.

On the day of her funeral, I had no idea the extent of the angers and resentments I was facing. It was like a lion's den. I showed up because I wanted to show my love and friendship and concern for her three children. I wanted to be supportive and helpful. It was like walking straight into the fire.

The funeral was a mess—utter chaos. There was no kind of organization, no privacy. There was an open casket, and the press and the public pushed their way in. It became a sideshow with gawking people everywhere. I felt embarrassed and deeply sad that there was no respect shown for Florence. The minimal security that had been hired showed little sensitivity to the day or the moment. I went straight for the kids. My greatest concern was to try to protect the children, but I was pushed around on every side by disrespectful, intrusive people. I was in a lot of emotional pain, but for a short time I tried to take charge. I guess it is my nature to try to be responsible and to organize chaos, but in this case maybe that was a bad thing to do. I got a lot of bad press for it later, but I only did it because I wanted to make things right for Florence. I finally gave up. I didn't go to the cemetery. I just got into my car feeling terrible and went home to grieve alone.

As I think back about our relationship, the worst of the resentments did not really come from Florence or from her mother. I thought Mrs. Ballard was a sweet and wonderful lady. I can almost hear her voice as I write about her; she was a heavyset woman, big, weighty. The trouble was never with her, it was with the other members of Florence's family, her brothers and sisters. I never really knew them, so I still don't understand why they spoke about me as if they knew me so well. I got heavily criticized for my part in the funeral. The truth is that I loved Florence, had no idea how bad things were for her, and I am still sad about her death.

Through the burden of my celebrity, I have learned certain ways to carry myself and my loads. I always try to see the bigger scheme of things and in so doing find a form of grace with which to live my life. I often see myself as the keeper of the flame, and this is how I felt about

Florence's light. I wanted to be the keeper of the flame for her. It doesn't always work. It seems that in this time of my life, it is most important for me to let go and get over any painful feelings that I have stuffed deep inside my heart. Maybe if I let them up and out, I can be free to have a happier life, to move to the next stages of my personal development, and to enjoy and take pleasure in my career as I did when we first began.

I remember my enthusiasm that summer before we got our contracts. When I needed a job to make some extra money, I asked Berry if I could work for him. He actually hired me as a secretary, probably because I was cute and persistent, but I wasn't really a secretary. All I remember doing was clearing off his desk several times a day, awed by the important-looking papers that he handled and so wishing to have my name on some of them. The Motown secretaries were something a little different. They all sang. They were mostly girls trying to break into the business. It was nothing out of the ordinary for me to take such a job. The other girls were fine with it. It was simply a summer job. I loved it. I was determined to do whatever it took to be close to the music.

103

Finally, at the beginning of 1961, our perseverance won out and our dreams came true. Berry Gordy decided to give us a recording contract. We were still a year away from graduating high school. We were beside ourselves with excitement; it was the most wonderful thing that had ever happened to us. Berry informed us that he didn't like the name "the Primettes." It would not do, and we couldn't use it. We needed to find a new name.

We thought about it for a long time, but we were not inspired. We just couldn't come up with the right one, so we each made a list. Still, nothing felt quite right. One day, when only Florence was in the studio, Janie Bradford, a great songwriter who was working at the Motown switchboard, handed her a list of what she considered good ideas. She told Florence that the contracts were being drawn up and she had to pick our name immediately. Florence picked "the Supremes" because it was the only one that didn't have an "ette" on the end. I hated the name then, but by the time we arrived at the studio, it was settled and already on the contracts.

I was only sixteen when we were called in to sign our contracts. We were all teenagers, and therefore, our parents were required to be present. In fact, they were really the ones who signed, as we were still under the legal age limit. It had always been a battle with Daddy, and this time was no exception. He was still dead set against my singing for a living, but after much pressure and pleading, he gave in, against his better judgment, of course. Although we girls were jumping out of our skins with enthusiasm, I recall the skepticism of all of our parents when we came together at Motown on that auspicious afternoon. They just didn't trust this little guy, Berry Gordy, not with our emotional development or with our money. Our enthusiasm was impossible to quell. We got what we wanted. We became Motown artists on January 15, 1961. Actually, we did our first recording for Berry on a label called Tamla under the organization of Berry Gordy Enterprises. He soon switched us to the Motown label, and every release after that was done for Motown.

In March 1961, we released a single called "I Want a Guy." I vividly remember this recording session. It felt so important. With my eyes closed and my arms outstretched, I poured my heart into this song. When I listen to it now, I feel nostalgic; I can hear that teenage yearning in my voice. Five months later we cut a song called "Buttered Popcorn" on which Florence sang lead. I don't know who wrote it, and I'm still trying to figure out what it was about:

> *My baby likes*
> *Buttered popcorn, uh-huh!*
> *Buttered popcorn, oh-hoh!*
> *It's sticky, oo-oey and gooey,*
> *Buttered popcorn.*

I don't think it meant anything. It was just about going to the drive-in movies. At that time, it was a big thing to be able to park outdoors on a warm summer night, put this sound box inside the window, and watch a movie on the big screen. Those were the days of making out at the drive-ins and dancing to music on skates at the roller rinks. It was all very cool.

My voice was very different then. I was quite nasal, but we had a good sound anyway. We were learning to blend. We never had actual voice lessons, but we got some help from a big, heavyset sweetheart of a guy named Maurice King. He was a dear man, and he used to tell us things like how to hit the right notes, how to avoid being flat or sharp, and how to make more interesting harmonies.

I wish we had had the opportunity to have formal voice training, but when we began singing professionally, singing lessons just weren't part of the program. As time went on, what motivated me to improve the quality of my voice was pure survival. I had to keep myself from getting hoarse or from losing my voice altogether. And so I was forced to start singing correctly, to sing from deep down in my diaphragm. I also began breathing correctly, not from a shallow place but from deeper within. I would take these full breaths and try to let the singing just come out of me. That's when my voice transformed. Again, Maurice King helped me, but we didn't get to spend much time with him. My new voice was basically self-taught. I learned from doing, the way I've accomplished most things in my life.

I have a special place in my heart for the old Hitsville building that Motown used for recording. We were convinced, like a lot of the other groups, that our unique sound came from the way our voices bounced off the walls and the windows. We recorded in every, and I mean every, nook and crevice of that building: the hallways, the stairwells, next to the walls, and even the toilet. We experimented in every way we could dream up. The hallway with the windows opened created a different sound than the hallways with the windows closed. When we sang next to one of the holes in the wall, that changed the sound, too. We were so inventive then; we had no synthesizers or electronics of any sort, so we would create sounds from whatever was around, like placing a bell on a chair and ringing it in different ways.

Have you ever sung in the shower and thought how good and interesting it sounded? There was a bathroom in the Hitsville building that happened to be located behind the control room, and it ended up being a perfect echo chamber. When I was doing leads, the engineers would sometimes put my microphone in the toilet to give my voice an echo effect. More of Berry's intuitive genius. I remember late one evening, when my throat hurt and I was weary and wanting to go home, finding myself singing my heart out beside the toilet bowl in that famous bathroom and thinking, "I guess show business isn't as glamorous as I thought it was."

Looking back, I can see that not only was Hitsville a great place to record, it had its own uniquely magical atmosphere. We all thought so, and nobody ever wanted to record anywhere else because that was where the hit sounds came from: from the holes in the walls, the stairwells, and the bathroom. And I really think there was a difference when we started recording at other more highly equipped professional studios. Hitsville carried a certain mystique, but in trying to maintain that mystique, producers would run the risk of creating rigidity. The attempt to reproduce certain sounds that had worked before or particular patterns for the placement of the instruments interfered with the creative process and generally didn't work out for the good of the project. When people believed that it was the studio itself that made the hits, they would want it set up in a certain way and then they wouldn't change it for fear that they might ruin the magic. The drums had to be in the far right-hand corner because the sounds would hit the wall in a particular way and then the mikes couldn't be moved. It was superstitious, as the music business often is, and nobody wanted to break the spell.

Way before Hitsville, USA, had earned its reputation, it was where the Supremes got their beginnings. It took a while. At first we released a lot of records that went nowhere, while new people who signed with the company after we did had hits galore. We were the youngest artists at Motown, the babies, and everybody referred to us as "the girls." We'd come to the studio right after school and record until the evening. It got dark early in Detroit, and we had to have a driver take us home. Everybody at Motown, including Smokey, our surrogate brother, and Berry himself, were always protecting us, taking care of the girls. Smokey and I were the best of friends, and we still are. Right from the start, Smokey was my mentor. He took a special interest in me, but he wasn't around that much. While the Supremes were breaking in, Smokey and the Miracles were becoming big stars. As a result, our friendship was elusive, only because he was on tour a lot. When he was in Detroit, he watched over us, making sure that we finished school, that we weren't out too late, that we got home safely.

Barbara Martin left the group in 1961, and the Supremes became a trio. Our first release under the Motown label was "Your Heart Belongs to Me," recorded in May of 1962. We did quite a few more, but nothing jived. We were frustrated, but we never gave up. In fact, up until "When the Lovelight Starts Shining Through His Eyes" in October of 1963, we didn't have a hit. That was our first one. That was the beginning.

"When the Lovelight Starts Shining Through His Eyes," which quickly went to the Top 20, had that real definable Motown sound. We had just started working with some songwriters called Holland-Dozier-Holland. Brian Holland had a strong gospel sense, and he was the one who worked out the part for the lead singer. Lamont Dozier was in charge of the harmonies and the background sounds, the music that goes beneath the lead to support her. And Eddie Holland created the performance level. Together they made an incredible triangle, just as the three of us did. Holland-Dozier-Holland became our main songwriters, and it was yet another great blend, another example of synergy that was a piece of the magic that was Motown at the time.

107

The relationship between the singers and the songwriters at Motown was unique. We all worked together as a single unit, so each song was created with a specific group in mind. The girls and I were fresh out of school; we were ready to explore the world with bright, eager eyes and wide-open hearts. When HDH looked at us, they must have seen our charm, our skinny bones, and our exuberant personalities. We were naive, and we gave off an innocence, a freshness. And so the songs that they created for us reflected that innocence, that naiveté. It's not that we were immune to the fact that the sixties were a time of great turbulence with the civil rights movement and Vietnam. It's not that we were disinterested in the protests and the rebellions that were exploding in the world around us then. It was quite the opposite; we were very interested and we cared, and in our own childlike way, we were contributing to the times. You see, although war and protest were the trademarks of the sixties, peace and love were the underlying fabric. The romantic quality of the innocent love songs that the Supremes became associated with were not only extremely well suited to our style, they were easy for people to understand and relate to. The synergy of the six of us, the singers and the songwriters, resulted in many classic songs that still hold up today. It was to be yet another year, in June of 1964 to be exact, when this superlative combination of singers and songwriters and the genius instincts of Berry Gordy would result in a #1 hit song.

I didn't know much about HDH as people, what they might have been experiencing in their personal lives and where they eventually ended up. Beyond the brilliant music they created, I have to admit that I didn't pay much attention to them. But then, I had little attention or energy to put out toward anyone then. It was a stressful time for us. We were young girls and had only started to work. We were so much into our own careers and just trying to make it, to keep our parents happy and worry-free so they wouldn't prevent us from continuing our dream. Then there were the everyday animosities and jealousies that inevitably surface in these kinds of situations along with the relentless and plain hard work required to build a successful career in show business.

Our lives were moving and changing at an incredible pace. It was difficult to focus on anything beyond ourselves, the present moment, and the immediate next step. We didn't exactly know what that next step was, but we knew we were headed somewhere big. I had a lot to guide and sustain me then: my direction, my determination, a commitment to hard work instilled by my family, and the support and encouragement of Berry Gordy, at times my surrogate father, at other times my controller and slave driver.

Diana, 1962.

Those Good Old Dreams

How do I begin to define my relationship with Berry, a connection that began when I was fifteen and, although it has completely altered, still exists today, some thirty-five years later? As all relationships do, ours went through many changes and took on various forms over the years. Sometimes Berry was a father to me, at other times a partner and cohort, and finally, at others, controlling and dominating. He and I could sail along on the identical wavelength, riding the surf so perfectly in communion that we left everybody else on the shore, or we could clash so dramatically that the treacherous seas we left in our wake would be hazardous for any craft. Berry was one of the most important men in my life when I was young. We went to some ecstatic places together, and then we could be shockingly out of touch. Even when I was deeply wounded by the startling lack of sensitivity he was capable of demonstrating, even when I felt unseen and emotionally abused, I always recognized him as an incomparable visionary, a dynamite character, a special human being.

Berry Gordy was raised tough. He was from a big family and was a boxer when he was young. At the same time, he had sensitivity, which he expressed through his great passion for music. I am told that in the early days he wrote songs for Jackie Wilson. Then, when he met Smokey Robinson, he was so impressed by his talents as a songwriter and a performer he decided to become a manager and go into business

OPPOSITE PAGE:
I'll never forget this poster. It was the first time we ever signed autographs.
A stranger ran up and asked you to sign your name on a piece of paper.
Yes, life had changed.

for himself. Berry's decision to manage Smokey was the big turn-around, the birth of his identity as a music mogul. I doubt that the shape of his new life surprised him. I think he always knew what he was capable of, even if nobody else did. He started Motown with eight hundred dollars that he borrowed from a family member. In five years, he had one of the hottest record companies in the country.

The Motown performers were creative and talented. We had a wonderful working relationship. Not only did Berry create a family atmosphere for us at Motown, he also gave us a solid foundation for the beginning of our careers. I don't know where Berry found this unique concept of how to go about building a business, but he did a fabulous job. These were good times. As I now approach fifty, I realize how magical those days really were. After thirty years of a rewarding and successful career, I realize how lucky I have been. When I began, I just wanted to sing for an audience, so I would have been a singer, even if nobody paid me. My career and my life were never about money or winning awards. My first dream was to be able to sing. My second dream was to be able to make a record. My third dream was to be able to perform onstage live. One by one, these dreams came true. Without Berry, they might not have. He assisted me in fulfilling my dreams and even helped me create new ones.

Berry's dad, Pops Gordy, was also a very special man whom I loved dearly. I was with him at a time when he was quite ill, and even then he had a special aura surrounding him. The Gordy family had a unique makeup of tough and loving. The women, Anna, Gwen, Esther, and even Mother Gordy, were powerful and strong at a time when few women were in their power. They were outspoken. My own family was a strong unit but in a different way. Berry always had a way of making things work for him. "Taking a negative and turning it into a positive," he used to say.

Unfortunately, Berry had a lot of run-ins with people. But Berry always won. When he turned on the charm, he was irresistible. Although I didn't know him in his youth, I expect he always had the ability to get what he wanted by knowing what was about to happen and acting on it with superb timing. In all our dealings throughout the years, he often behaved as a control freak and a kind of dictator, but he was never simple or narrow-minded. He was a genius, open to abundant possibilities. He could plan for the future based on the larger scope of things. He never thought small. No matter how difficult the challenge, he could envision and hold on to the big picture, and he had little time or patience for anyone who couldn't go there with him.

Before he became successful, he used to expound endlessly upon many of his brilliant ideas, and his sisters would say to him, "If you're so smart, why aren't you a millionaire?" He would look over at them and say quite calmly, "Just wait." He knew something they didn't know, and it didn't really bother him whether or not they supported his vision. He just kept right on dreaming and making his plans. He would not be deterred.

Even in our first audition, Berry Gordy must have recognized something special in us. I'm certain that if he hadn't, he would never have allowed us to hang around Hitsville every day. Nothing went on without his permission, even if it was unspoken. Berry was decidedly the boss, and everyone knew it. Although he appeared to be constantly occupied and basically removed from our comings and goings, he most assuredly was watching us. We would never have been called on or allowed to sing backup for his established artists, nor would the others in the company have taken to us so totally, if Berry had not given his blessing. Although we were frustrated a great deal and wondered if we would ever get what we truly wanted, this waiting game was an important period in our development. We may not have been aware of what we were actually doing, but in hindsight I can see that it was during this time, before we were signed, that we were getting our act together. Although the refining process took on greater proportions after our first big hit and continued on all throughout our career, we had already begun creating that special sound and look that was uniquely ours.

I had always been good at doing hair, I really enjoyed it. I remember that my mother had been adept at using the curling irons, and I must have picked it up from her. Mama taught me to heat them up by putting them on top of the stove or over the gas fire. I practiced on myself and learned to twist and turn those curlers and have them literally dancing in my hands. I would go through the magazines or watch television, and then I'd copy the styles that I particularly liked. I took great pride in my work. I knew how to tease hair, brush it on top, and then make it stand way out. I loved doing French braids, and I learned to make another kind of braid that we called a "plat," and I'd slick it down with some strange-smelling stuff called Dixie Peach. I liked doing hair so much I'd work on anybody in the neighborhood who came to me, and sometimes I made a little extra change that way.

I used to have a great time practicing on Mary and Florence, particularly when we were refining the look for the Supremes. Mary's hair was easy enough to manage, but part of Florence's mystique was her soft, thin hair, unusual for a black woman. I took it on as a challenge, first using the straightening comb and then the curlers. We had fun, and she always ended up looking great.

Another part of our signature look was the beautiful gowns we wore. Even as teenagers, we had a sense of sophistication that made us stand out from other performers. Nobody created that look for us; we did it ourselves. We brought it to Motown. None of the girls in the other groups wore gowns like ours, at least not until we introduced that fashionable evening look. It was natural to us because one of the things that we all shared was our love of elegance. We took great pleasure in wearing beautiful gowns, jewelry, and shoes; we always looked like young ladies. More influence from my mother. Once again, the things that I learned from her became an integral part of who the Supremes came to be. How fitting that when we embarked on our first tours, she should travel with us as chaperon.

Before we had a budget to work with, the three of us would put our money together. Mary and I would buy elegant fabrics, and then we'd look through magazines to choose designs that attracted us. Once we had decided what we wanted, I would spend days cutting and sewing our stage outfits in the likeness of the ads. I remember when those wild balloon dresses were in style. They really appealed to us, so I made some flowered ones that we stuffed with crinolines to create this big bell at the bottom.

Although Berry Gordy contributed to our choices of songs and our direction, I can't really give him any credit for the sophisticated elegance that we embodied. Or for the self-esteem, morals, and standards that we had. That's who we already were. Berry Gordy did not have to "create" young ladies from ghetto teens, like some inner-city Eliza Doolittles. We were already ladies who had been brought up right. These fine qualities were already ours, instilled in us by our upbringing and our families. It was what he already saw in us that Berry helped us develop, these natural qualities that he began to nurture and pull together. After we became a success, Berry started forcing his other girls at the company to pull it together and to have standards to live up to. We definitely started it. Our attitudes and our looks were organic to us, and Berry was smart enough to see that and to work with what was already there. Many things that have been written give the impression that he made us from nothing. That was not the case.

We worked hard throughout 1963, making lots of recordings, including our first album, *Meet the Supremes*. On the original release of this album, we wore exquisite dresses I had made. I took great pride in them and considered these handmade outfits to be the very height of fashion. Few people ever saw that version of the album cover because after we hit the charts big the next year, Berry decided to rerelease the album with a new cover photo that was shot closer in so you could really see our faces.

In April 1964 we recorded "Where Did Our Love Go." The Supremes had had a string of singles that weren't successful, but Berry hadn't given up on us. The Marvelettes and Martha and the Vandellas had come on board at Motown after we did and had hits before us. Even when we felt discouraged with ourselves, Berry continued to believe in us. If I have someone who truly believes in me, I can move mountains. Between my mother's faith and the way Berry Gordy stayed true to his vision, I kept on trying.

"Where Did Our Love Go" wasn't scheduled to be released until sometime in the summer. In the meantime, they had booked us on a tour called "Dick Clark's Caravan of Stars." We were only twenty years old at the time, and we desperately wanted to be included. There were so many big names, and we wanted to be among them. Somehow, Berry

Gordy succeeded in booking us on that tour, but we were not mentioned separately in any of the press releases. The ads read, "Gene Pitney! The Shirelles! Brenda Holloway! and Others!" That was us—"Others."

Before we left, Berry Gordy's sister, Esther Edwards, who worked at Motown, called us into her office. She wanted us to know how lucky we were, that they had to beg just to get us on the tour, that we were really there only for filler. I didn't care. Besides my Southern trip and our trip to Canada to compete in that talent contest, we hadn't been anywhere and we barely knew there was a world outside of the one in which we had been raised.

As a kid growing up in a small neighborhood, all you know and all you hear are the family sounds that expand beyond the paper-thin walls of the apartment next door. We knew there were other worlds to explore, beautiful homes in certain parts of Detroit where blacks didn't live because we couldn't afford to. And there were only certain schools we could attend. I wanted more. I wanted to see the face of America, to see other aspects of life. I was eager for experience, and I was ready for whatever life had in store, to ride the wind.

It was "Dick Clark's Caravan of Stars" that my mother—our chaperon—was affectionately dubbed "Mama Supreme." It was sometimes difficult to be a twenty-year-old traveling with her mother, but the tour was hard and Mama was special, so I mostly loved it. It certainly made things better with Daddy. He couldn't come to terms with his young daughter's dressing up in gowns and wearing makeup. "Why do you have all that black stuff around your eyes?" he would ask. I guess he had a point because when we were still teenagers, we were already wearing makeup, trying to look grown-up. As I think back, when he saw his sixteen-year-old daughter leaving the house for a performance with teased-up hair and makeup on her face, how could he be sure she was doing the right thing? He wasn't sure he trusted Berry anyway. So when I went on the road and Mama went along, it relieved some of the pressure because Daddy was much more accepting. It seemed that Mama trusted me more than he did.

Mama had a positive personality, and everybody liked having her around. She was warm and loving with us girls, but she was also firm. She had incredible standards. She was a real stickler for cleanliness and organization. Whenever we stayed in hotels, she always used to say, "Leave the hotel room just like you found it." So we made up our beds each morning before we got back on the bus. She taught us how to pack our bags properly, too. I don't know how she knew all these things. But she did. I remember how she used to pull out my drawers when I was growing up, and if they were messy, she'd just dump them all out on the floor and we'd start from scratch. I should probably do that to my daughters, but as much as I try to emulate some of Mama's ways, I'm not as strict as she was. I try to be an example of the right way to live, but I'm more relaxed and I think that people should basically be comfortable. And yet my mother is the most positive role model that ever showed up in my life. Even as strict as she was when we were on tour, I think all the girls would agree that she had more class than anyone we had ever met. Period. And she was a great help during some very frightening, confusing, and difficult times.

In some of those Southern towns, you could just feel the bigotry in the air. You could slice it with a knife like stinking cheese. Sometimes we were afraid to get off the bus and ask where the toilet was. There were many times we would stop at a café or gas station and were not allowed to use the public rest rooms. We had to squat beside the bus and pee in the bushes.

I think the most frightening experience of all happened in Macon, Georgia. Late one night after a performance, a sniper shot at us as we were leaving the concert hall. At that time, it was strict segregation in Georgia. We used to try to integrate the audiences. When we heard the shots, we took off toward the bus as quickly as we could. We tore up the stairs of that bus so fast people fell into the aisles and rolled on top of each other. When we got far enough away for our hearts to stop pounding, we saw that the shots had gone right through the metal, hit the glass window, and the entire front of the bus was full of tiny shotgun pellets.

Even with these problems and obstacles, what remains foremost in my mind is the positive experience of that tour, the fun of all of us being together, the pure joy of going onstage every night and singing with the Supremes.

When the tour began, we were the opening act. The more popular and successful the group, the later on in the evening it appeared, so the name acts were the closers. As the summer wore on, "Where Did Our Love Go," which had been released in June while we were already traveling, started gaining popularity. At first we were so busy riding the bus and performing we were unaware of what was happening with our record. But the audiences knew. They began to recognize us. They would scream and shout when we appeared onstage, and when we got to the wings we'd scream to each other, "They know our song! They're out there dancing to our song!" As our record slowly but surely climbed the charts, we were coming on later and later in the show. I'll never forget the thrill of riding on the bus, being halfway across the country from Detroit and hearing our song played on the radio. We would flip the dials and try to find out which stations were playing it. Sometimes when we made our pit stops in some small town, we'd run to a newsstand to find a copy of *Billboard* or *Cash Box* to see where we stood on the charts. All of the things that I had dreamed when I had first heard Smokey's song on the radio were happening to us. The dream was coming true.

By the end of the summer, we had the number one song in the country and we were headlining the show. Imagine it, in one summer we had gone from being the openers, the bottom of the barrel, to being the most popular group. It seemed impossible to believe that our group was now being billed above Gene Pitney. When the tour was over, we returned to Motown triumphant, with stars in our eyes. Our future dreams had become our present reality. We were finally on our way.

Get Up and
Sit on the Piano

W hen we finished the Dick Clark tour and returned to Detroit, everything had changed. We recorded "Baby Love" and "Come See About Me" that year, so along with "Where Did Our Love Go" we had three consecutive number one hits. The Supremes had made it. Everybody knew about us and knew that we could sing. As performers, we still needed polishing. We had some major work to do. And I, for one, was ready and eager.

Berry put us into a program that he created for Motown called "Artistic Development." It was like attending finishing school to learn valuable things they didn't teach you at Northeastern or Cass Technical High School. Little things like etiquette, things a girl would not learn while she was growing up in the projects. That teaching was infinitely valuable then and still is today. Motown was fine-tuning an instrument.

Maxine Powell, who had originally been a model and then went on to become a modeling teacher, was one of my most important influences at that time. There were so many little things that she gave us. When we started wearing miniskirts, it added a whole new set of problems, like sliding out of a car like a lady. Maxine taught us how to get in and out of an automobile gracefully. Then there were times when we were singing with a band and someone would say, "Get up and sit on the piano!" There was a graceful way to do that, too, to glide up there. It was Maxine Powell who showed me how to do it without looking phony. We

OPPOSITE PAGE:
In those days, there was a strange kind of magic flowing through the air.
Everything was happening so fast.

giggled a lot about this, but when we had finished her training, we could sit at the table with Princess Margaret or Princess Anne and feel at ease. We could look and feel as if we belonged anywhere. Maxine was a very special person, and she greatly contributed to my increased self-confidence.

Another aspect of our artistic development was working with Cholly Atkins, a wonderful and talented choreographer. He worked mostly with Mary and Florence, as they needed to smooth out the background steps. Since I sang the leads, I was in the position to play the audience. I was given the space to walk from here to there as my mood and the energy of the song moved me. Mary and Florence had much more rigid dance routines since they had to stay behind their mikes. Cholly Atkins taught them what to do.

In a certain sense, I was winging it, for there was no one around to show me how to act as a lead singer and there was no way to watch myself. There weren't any monitors and there was no video then, so you couldn't practice your act, watch your performance, see what needed changing, and then go back and do it again. There were no mirrors or reflections to study. In those days, most of it, like *The Ed Sullivan Show,* was live. Our career was hands-on. Our education came from traveling, and our experience came from doing. People like Maurice King, Maxine Powell, and Cholly Atkins were our only mirrors. And of course Berry Gordy was always there.

Berry would sit in the audience with a large legal pad, taking detailed notes, and then come backstage after every performance and tell us what we did wrong. He always had notes: Tighten up the act, you sang this wrong, you girls weren't moving together, you weren't smiling, and on and on. The information was helpful, it was always geared toward improving our act, but Berry behaved like a tyrant and his way of talking about our performance and pointing these things out was heavily judgmental, discouraging, and ultimately very hard on us.

We weren't Berry's sole focus. He tried to improve everybody's performance. He often had notes for the lighting people and the musicians. Everybody resisted him because of his rough style. Berry really liked Sammy Davis, Jr.'s shows, so he would study them and find things that were especially smooth, like the way Sammy snapped his fingers and the lights went out. He would bring that stuff to me and the lighting people and have us practice together. Then sometimes he would escort me to Sammy's shows in Vegas so that I could watch and learn. I also remember going to Bobby Darin's shows because Berry thought Bobby was a great performer.

Berry mostly concentrated his attention on the Supremes; there is no doubt about that. He gave a lot to Smokey in the early days, but more at the beginning. The other acts said he didn't spend any time with them because of me. He was like the father, and everybody wanted his attention. Everybody wanted him to come to see their shows. I remember when he couldn't make it to a show and he would send a wire, GOOD SHOW or GO BREAK A LEG. Whoever was performing on that particular night would be really upset and give him a hard time. "You didn't come to the show? How could you miss it?" And then when he *was* there and he came crashing backstage with a multitude of notes and corrections, we all resented the criticism because he was too hard on us. His forceful style only created animosities. Everybody wanted his attention, but nobody liked what he had to say. It must have been hard for him. I guess he was really being dragged all over, but he loved being the boss. We never thought much about that then. He came across as powerful and in control. His lack of sensitivity with the others created a lot of problems for me.

Berry wasn't careful of people's feelings, and his dominating manner antagonized us. It was like parents making you study. You might be getting better and smarter, but it was too punishing and you ended up hating them for it. That was how we all felt toward Berry. He was the leader and everybody wanted his focus and approval, but he played favorites and set up an unhealthy internal climate. He used to say things to the other performers like "Why can't you be more like Diana? She makes her plans, she works really hard, she rehearses all day long, and she records all night. Why can't you be like her?" Comparing is a terrible thing to do in a family situation. If you have three kids and single out one of them and keep saying to the others, "Why can't you be like her?" it produces crippling sibling rivalry. I feel that was how it all

123

started, and it became a very difficult situation for me. Everybody worked hard, and everybody did things in her own way. When they were not recognized or when they were compared to me, they turned not only on Berry but also on his chosen one. I think that's what happened to me. I became the "good" child, the object of Dad's affection, and everyone turned against me. I lived under constant stress. I was the object of everybody's jealousy then. I bore the brunt of a lot of blame. I am quite clear that I am not responsible for anybody else's successes or failures. All I know is I worked hard all the time. This was a place where Berry and I connected, where we were the same.

After our initial success, it was as if we were charmed, and we kept on recording hits. The year after "Where Did Our Love Go" sold two million copies, we had a string of five more hits, including "Stop! In the Name of Love," "Back in My Arms Again," and "I Hear a Symphony." Motown had a great drummer, Benny Benjamin, who played for us. In fact, he played on almost every record that came out of Motown and was partially responsible for that driving Motown sound. Holland-Dozier-Holland were still composing for us, and we became the only singing group to have six consecutive gold records in one year.

I will never forget the first time we worked at the Copacabana. I did our makeup and hair, and this was the first time we ever signed autographs. I stood there in amazement, holding a piece of paper that someone had asked me to sign, knowing for certain that life had changed. I was so grateful. I still cannot think of a better way to have spent my life. It is still so gratifying to be a singer and a performer, to be able to make movies, to see an idea completed in a song or a video, to participate in the writing of a script, and, even now, to be writing my memoirs. This is a beautiful life.

And those sixties television shows! I remember the excitement and the tension as we got ready for *Shindig, Hullabaloo,* and Dick Clark's *American Bandstand.* Just think about it—a kid from the Brewster projects suddenly doing television shows that are being shown all over the world.

The people who were in and out of Hitsville in those good old days, the fabulous stars who comprised the Motown family, were some of the most superb people I have ever known. It was an honor to be a part of such an exciting family. We had a grand kind of togetherness. The names are endless: Janie Bradford, Faye Hale, Gil Askey, Marv Johnson, Barrett Strong, John O'Den. These are some of the creatively talented people behind the scenes who are responsible for making the stars and the hits. Hal Davis was another one. Berry's brothers and sisters George, Robert, Fuller, Esther, and Gwen worked in the organization to make it a better place.

There have always been incredible artists at Motown, especially in the early days: the Funk Brothers, Earl Van Dyke, Beans Bowles, the Four Tops, and Gladys Knight. I liked Gladys very much; I admired her stage work, her presence, and her talent. We were all directed by Berry, who put these units together, and we all loved being there. Each group was unique, and we needed the direction. Martha and the Vandellas had their special sound, the Temptations, the Marvelettes, and the Miracles had theirs, and we had ours. Although we shared some of the same songwriters and the same musicians, we each had our special songs with a different kind of feel. Berry saw to that.

I had a lot of feeling for Marvin Gaye, particularly in the later years. He was such a talented man, but he had so many personal problems and he seemed so confused. I think he desperately needed some support and guidance, but he didn't give people a chance. I remember sitting at the piano with Marvin once when he was writing a song. He was in such despair, and the words came out like this:

> Oh, my baby,
> You treat me so mean.
> Oh, oh, oh,
> I believe I'll commit suicide.

This was during the late sixties, a time when he was deeply depressed. I believe that his pain and unhappiness were the cause of his death. What a tremendous tragedy for a parent to murder his own child!

Mary Wells was another great talent. She was leaving the company when we were getting started, so I don't remember much about her. I

125

think it was a pity that she left Motown at the height of her big hit record. Although I hardly knew her, I was very sad when I heard she had cancer.

I miss Eddie Kendricks, who also recently died of cancer, and I miss David Ruffin. I hate losing special people who are part of my history, but life goes on. When I sing "Missing You," it's not only about Marvin. I think of my mother, Florence, Paul, Eddie, and David.

Over the years, my relationship with Stevie Wonder has grown and blossomed. Today, he feels like my brother. I remember when he first came to Motown with his bongos, a genius talent. I respected his song-writing so much. I begged and begged him to write something for me. He finally did. It was a terrific song called "The Force Behind the Power." There is a tremendous message in that song, and I believe that it will last forever in my career and in my heart. To me, Berry Gordy was the force behind the power of that world and those days.

Suzanne de Passe, who became a powerful Motown producer, was my closest friend. She discovered Lionel Richie. She nurtured the Commodores, she brought them to Motown, and she got Berry to sign them. She was also influential in the careers of the Jacksons. People cherish her friendship as I do because she takes time and attention with people. She is a good listener, and she really cares about people, often more than she cares about herself. Due to her relationship with Berry, she has been able to start her own company. Of course she was a very talented woman, a success in her own right, but Berry brought her a long way.

I saw Quincy Jones a few days ago, and it brought to mind the power of recording "We Are the World," that amazing song he produced and Michael Jackson and Lionel Richie cowrote to raise money for people starving in Africa and the United States. It was so wonderful to be involved in an experience in which many artists came together to support each other. It was a special moment in history, and it reminded me of the days at Motown when we were a family. I recently gave a speech for the Global Youth Forum at the United Nations. At the end of my speech, a kid came up onto the stage with a microphone and started singing, "We Are the World." The entire audience joined in, and we were united.

As the Supremes became more and more popular, we knew that along with how hard we were working and the magic we were creating, we were also lucky. We had a strong life force, and things just happened for us. Dick Clark took a special liking to us and wanted us on his shows, which contributed a great deal to maintaining our popularity. We were wanted, and Berry utilized our fame to his advantage. Sometimes he would make a deal: "Okay. You can have the Supremes, but you'll also have to take one of our newer acts that is coming up." Berry wanted us all to help each other; he wanted what was good for the entire Motown family.

The rewards of our realized dream were fabulous. I loved the entire process, and I was so happy just to be able to sing, just to be able to perform, to be able to travel, and to have my singing be a serious profession, not just a hobby. Getting my passport to Europe and knowing that I was about to see the world was such a thrill. I was always grateful. The highs were high, but the tension that accompanied them and the work that was required to maintain our performance quality during the recording and extensive touring was overwhelming and debilitating. I continued anyway; I've never been afraid of hard work.

Sometimes the stress got so bad I couldn't eat. I just couldn't swallow anything. I'd put the food in my mouth, but my jaws would clamp together and I couldn't chew. It got so that I couldn't even tolerate the smell of food. It was too pungent for me. Perhaps it was a form of anorexia. I was becoming skin and bones, and eating became repulsive. It was a very unhappy time for me. Most of the kids I knew who were my age were out having a good time, dancing, dating, spending time with their boyfriends, but I was just working. I felt out of touch, out of control. Although the Supremes were at the top, I often felt as if I were sitting at the bottom of a deep, dark pit. It was no fun.

Berry was very worried about me. Even though he had a rough style, he also had a caring, sensitive side to him. He did everything he could to take care of me. I remember performing in Chicago when the chill factor was well below zero and the piercing wind had no mercy as it ripped around the street corners. There is no place that feels colder than Chicago in winter. When I got offstage each night, I was in a cold sweat and having chills, so Berry rubbed down my arms, legs, and feet with alcohol and covered me up so I wouldn't catch a cold. At those times, I really felt that he loved me.

He often seemed to know what to do to help because he related to me. I guess he could see himself in me. I think that the greatest connection between Berry and me was our powerful life energy; we both had it. Perhaps it is presumptuous of me to refer to our similarities back in the early days, for I was just a child and my own development was just beginning. As time went on and the work became more intense, this zest and passion for the work and for life became evident in both of us. We could go on and on when everybody else fell by the wayside, and we each loved seeing that energetic embrace of life reflected in the other.

Once I was so stressed out, I got an angry skin rash; I broke out with blotches all over my body. It was just nerves. In actuality, I was a nervous wreck when I was with the Supremes. Our schedules were grueling, and I never had enough sleep. My shoulders were always tight. I used to carry them high, right up to my neck. It got so bad Berry was often at a loss to know what to do for me. I remember that once he flew my brother Chico in to see me because he thought it would make me happy. He was always trying to make me eat, which made me even more nervous. He wanted to make me strong so that I could keep going onstage and singing, but I kept getting skinnier and skinnier.

As I think back on this time, it brings tears to my eyes. It was so incredibly stressful, and I'm trying to figure out why. I guess it was the demand of performing and the fear of not being good enough. It was the pressure of trying to do everything right for everybody else and losing myself in the Supremes and in the process.

In those days, when we were doing "the Motor Town Revue," for example, we would do five or six shows a day. They were short shows in which we performed only one or two songs, but they went on all day long, so there was never any time to rest or simply enjoy our success. We played what we called the Chitlin Circuit, theaters like the Apollo in New York, the Regal in Washington, D.C., and the Royal in Baltimore. We worked with Frankie Lymon and the Teenagers, the Shirelles, Otis Redding, O. C. Smith, all the stars who were around at that time. My mother wasn't with us then, but we always had a chaperon, a lady who made sure that after we finished the shows we got into our car and arrived safely back at the hotel. I think the Apollo was my favorite because there used to be these steak houses down the street where you could go out between performances and have delicious steak sandwiches and baked potatoes. For some reason, they were really appealing to me, one of the few meals I enjoyed eating. Even with that, even as much as I enjoyed performing, the stress was not relieved because there was the perpetual pressure of doing it right for Berry. He was so relentlessly demanding. Even when he wasn't there, we felt the need to get it right.

He used to love to put us on the spot and embarrass us, even after we had gained great commercial success. Perhaps it was premeditated, his way of maintaining control over us. We would just happen to walk into a room where he was talking with some industry people and he would snap his fingers and say, "Okay, girls, stand over there and do this song. Any song. Just do it a cappella. C'mon, c'mon. Just do it!" And we'd start in, "Gray skies are gonna clear up, put on a happy face." We'd just do it. Once when we were in Japan he and I had a meeting with some powerful promoters. Berry, in his inimitable fashion, suddenly turned to me and said, "Just sing the song!" Intimidated and dreadfully uncomfortable, I heard a tiny little speaking voice come out of me and say, "Well, I've never really sung this song without music, but I'll try." And I did it, sang the song on the spot, without music.

Then there was *The Ed Sullivan Show*. The producers wanted us to do our biggest hit at the time, but Berry had a different idea. He wanted people to know that we could also sing show tunes. So Berry started doing what he did best, making a deal. Bob Precht was the *Ed Sullivan* producer, and Berry said to him, "Okay. We'll let you have this number one record, but at the same time you have to let them do one of their standard songs." And we had to get up once again and spontaneously sing something a cappella for Bob Precht. Berry nearly always got what he wanted, but at our expense.

It was a hard time then, a public time. We were whisked in and out of cars and tour buses, and we were constantly being probed and interviewed about all the facets of our lives. And yet my time with the

129

Supremes, as stressful and difficult as it was, lives in my mind as a positive experience. One of the things that I am most proud of is the fact that the Supremes were trailblazers, both as women and black artists.

When I first began my career, while we were traveling through the South, I didn't know who was buying the music. Even then, although unaware, we were already crossing color lines and breaking racial barriers. When you think about it, music is a perfect way to accomplish this because people don't see the color of your skin when they listen to the radio. So our tours through the South, as dangerous and scary as they were, ended up serving a higher purpose: Since both blacks and whites were listening to, loving, and enjoying the music, we were actively changing the world by doing what we loved best—singing.

There were some radio stations that would only play white singers like Pat Boone. Or cover singers like Elvis Presley, who performed black musicians' songs. There were also some very courageous DJs who were extremely influential then, who contributed to the cause. These men loved our sound and began to play a lot of the Motown music. They were the pioneers, the ones who inspired and paved the way for the other radio stations to start playing black music. So we were a part of the change and the breaking-out process. As I've grown older, I have learned that the more you believe in yourself, the more you can develop an internal power source, out of which comes the strength to choose a positive outlook on life. And so, as I think back, my true vision of being a Supreme is a joyful one. I could certainly choose to focus on the negative. There were hard times, tremendous pressures, and difficult personality clashes. But those are not my most prominent memories. What I remember best is the ability to have a career doing what I loved best, the good fortune to be connected to an extended family in a wonderful creative atmosphere, and finally the opportunity to learn from a clever and powerful visionary who did the best for us that he knew how to do.

It was with the Supremes that I first had the chance to travel through Europe. It was such a great opportunity for me then, and I have spent a lot of time there during the last ten years. I like how I feel when I'm there. I appreciate the sense of equality and freedom without the unspoken prejudice that is present in America. I can understand why so many performers traveled to Europe in the early days and decided to live there. It was how the Europeans made them feel: special and important. I remember reading that Josephine Baker felt special in Europe that she was able to rise above the negativity of prejudice against the color of her skin. She was able to mix with royalty on an equal basis. They respected her as a human being, not just as someone who performed for them.

I have been all over Europe, and almost all of it feels good, whether it's Germany, England, Italy, or, especially, France. The food is wonderful, and Paris is such a romantic place. I spent a year living there when I was working on a film about Josephine Baker, and I put my girls in the French-American school there. Europe was an opportunity that I would never have had if I had not been a Supreme.

I view my life as a Supreme as positive, not because I am in denial or overlooking the difficulties. I know they were there. But I faced them, lived through them, learned from them, and transformed them. In the final analysis, I see that amazing time as a positive one because I decided to make it that way, and so it was. My dream was fulfilled.

DIANA ROSS & THE SUPREMES

Farewell

THE LAST PERFORMANCE. RECORDED LIVE AT THE FRONTIER HOTEL, LAS VEGAS, JANUARY 14, 1970.

MOTOWN®
5C 038-91710

Going Through Changes

M ary, Florence, and I were not true sisters. Other groups like the Ronettes and the Jackson Five were actually blood relatives and had been brought up together in the same house. The girls and I started out as three strangers who were randomly placed together. Mary and Florence had already been friends for a short while when I was brought in, so I was the new girl who was introduced into this already existing unit. I think we did very well together considering the fact that we had just met. When difficulties arose, we did not have the kind of bond that automatically exists among family members. We didn't have the kind of commitment or understanding that no matter what happened, we were together forever. We discussed this; we tried to treat it like a club. You be the president, you be the vice president, I'll be the secretary, and when things come up, we'll just work it out within that context. This was effective at first, but when the energy escalated, it just didn't work anymore.

Changes are organic to life experience, so when I look back, it is no surprise that changes occurred within the Supremes. All things considered, it was actually quite natural, but when change happens, it is a human characteristic to resist that change and to wonder what went wrong. Really, nothing went wrong. The shifting was all in the natural scheme of things. Under normal circumstances, change is viewed as inevitable and for the good of progress. The circumstances of our lives

OPPOSITE PAGE:
Sweet love and tenderness.
All our hopes and dreams will take us through the hard times.

were far from normal. When the momentum of our success really got moving, it blew in like a wild hurricane. In our attempt to keep grounded, we lost perspective.

When we were first trying to break into music, we spent all our afternoons and late into the nights rehearsing, trying to follow directions, trying to be the best that we could be. At that time, we all dreamed the same dream: of being singers. We never knew that singing would be so much work. And then, when it suddenly went from frustration and nothing to success and everything, it all happened too fast. The stress of that degree of fame at such young ages took its toll on all of us. I have already spoken about how the stress was affecting me, and although Mary had tremendous inner strength, it took all she had to keep it going. In retrospect, I see that it was hardest on Florence. Although she appeared strong and hardy, that was obviously only how it looked on the outside. Her inner constitution was quite tenuous and imbalanced.

By the mid-sixties, life was becoming very difficult. We were basically living out of suitcases, touring endlessly, doing one-nighters all across the country, and recording albums, laced with touring through Europe. It was very tough to maintain the stamina to keep going. You had to love singing so much, you had to want it so bad, in order to work at it that hard. Florence loved to sing, but she just didn't seem to be able to keep up with the lifestyle. She was always tired and angry, and eventually, the pressure became too much for her.

I feel sad about what happened to her because my early memories of Florence are of a beautiful, wonderful girl. Her manner was so naturally regal that she carried her head high. People often mistook that attitude for snobbishness and unkindness, but they were wrong. They had simply misjudged her. In her heart, she was a good person. When she began to fall apart, it was tragic.

I can't remember exactly when she started drinking, but it was sometime during the period of constant touring. At first, it was beer, but after a while, that wasn't enough to drown out her own pain. She went on to hard liquor. Often, when we went out onstage, she would be completely out of it and it seemed as if she just didn't care. I'll never forget a show we did at the Flamingo Hotel in Las Vegas. Mary and I were thrilled to be there, it was one of the places that we never imagined at the beginning of our careers we'd get the chance to play. But here we were, as excited as we could be, and then Florence showed up, late and drunk. Our costumes were tuxedos. Florence had gained so much weight, her stomach was bulging out of her costume. We were embarrassed to go onstage with her.

There were times that she'd miss recording sessions and even shows. She just wouldn't show up, and we didn't know where she was or what she was doing. I remember once we suddenly realized at show time that Florence hadn't arrived. Mary and I were frantic; we ended up having to go on without her. We abandoned the regular choreography, and, after grabbing the hand mikes, we walked around the stage and sang, just the two of us. She was constantly letting us down. These were stress-filled days for all of us, but they were also times of great accomplishment and rewards. We had larger opportunities than ever before. We wanted to be able to enjoy it all, but Florence's mood swings were dramatic and she ruined it for everyone. I was giving as much of myself as I possibly could, and Mary was also a hard worker. It was difficult enough to stay centered and cope with the touring, the stress of performing every night, the massive publicity, and the exhaustion. If that wasn't enough, whatever energy we had left was being drained by Florence's moods and inconsistencies.

135

During that time, I recorded "Someday We'll Be Together," a wonderful song by Johnny Bristol. The reason I say "I recorded" is that, although no one knew it at the time, the girls were not my backup singers. I guess this will destroy a lot of illusions, but the girls were not even at that session. We couldn't get them there, and a couple of other girls did it. Things were not the same. I was beginning to be singled out very pointedly. Changes were in the air.

Florence was not well, she had serious emotional problems, but we didn't know that then. We just saw her as an angry woman who drank too much and wouldn't take responsibility for herself. She blamed everyone else for the things that were not working out in her life. When we were getting lots of press that started to mention only my name, it was difficult for her. The articles would refer to "the skinny little girl who . . . ," and that hurt her very much. She started acting out in a big way, and Berry soon became aware of how bad things were.

One night in Las Vegas, while I was talking to Berry on the phone, he heard a commotion. Florence was drunk, and she was yelling and carrying on. "What's going on out there?" he wanted to know. I didn't want to tell him how drunk Florence was, but before I could try to protect her, she grabbed the phone out of my hand and said, "Who is it? Who is on this phone?" Berry heard her voice and knew immediately what was going on. He jumped on the next plane to Vegas. He wanted to know the full extent of what was happening and to see if he could do something about it.

Nothing could be done. I think it was even out of Florence's control. In retrospect, her depression was more than just a mood, it was obviously something medical. It was no longer possible for the group to go on as before. At the beginning of 1967, by mutual consent, Florence left the group. Although we were very sad that things hadn't worked out with Florence, we also breathed a sigh of relief. We were tired of having to cope with her moods and trying to take care of her.

Here was the possibility for a new beginning, but we had immediate commitments for the Supremes and we were minus one singer. We had to fill the space right away. Cindy Birdsong had been singing with Patti LaBelle and the Bluebells when we approached her. She was the same physical size as Florence, all the costumes fit her, she sang in the same key, and they had similar personas. When she first joined us, she was rather intimidated and sang very quietly. None of us really expected her to stay on as a Supreme; we thought that she was coming in as a filler for a while and then she would return to her former group. But it turned out very differently. She ended up staying on until I left three years later. The pressure was on Mary, who spent many rehearsal hours showing her the moves that they were to do together. I remember Cindy as a sweet, pleasant girl, anxious to please.

As we formed our new group, Berry took this opportunity to make an additional change. A separation had been brewing for a long time. In my opinion, it was a forced separation, one largely created by outside influences. I had been singing all the leads, and so the press had been singling me out from the other two girls. And then there were the fans. Instead of appreciating us as a unit, they kept picking out their favorite Supreme, saying this one was better than that one, thereby pitting us against each other. In mid-1967, Berry officially changed the name of our group to "Diana Ross and the Supremes." This was not my idea. It came from Berry. He discussed it in detail with Mary and me. It seemed inevitable. He explained to us that it would also be easier to demand more salary if we were a lead singer and a group. Instead of the pressure lifting, it only increased. Something had to give.

A Wild Ride

With Cindy Birdsong as the newest Supreme, we once again hit our stride. We never restored the harmony and excitement present when we first began, but over the next few years, Diana Ross and the Supremes were able to carry on, performing and recording some wonderful hits. Holland-Dozier-Holland wrote many of them for us. When they finally made the decision to leave Motown, Berry put us with some new songwriters who wrote some different music for us. Among these songs were "Love Child" in September of 1968 and "I'm Livin' in Shame" in January of 1969. I enjoyed these new songs, they had a wonderful sound, but for me they weren't as wonderful as the older HDH love songs like "Baby Love" and "Stop! In the Name of Love." These were the oldies that had been written especially for us. These new songs were about somebody else's life, so when I sang them, it was like doing an audio movie. They would make great videos today. "Love Child," a song about a child born out of wedlock, was the first controversial topic with which we ever dealt. "I'm Livin' in Shame" was supposed to be a girl singing about her mother ("cookin' bread with a dirty raggedy scarf hangin' 'round her head"). The lyrics were good, but those sweet romantic love songs like "Come See About Me" were more real to me. It was the sixties. Life was moving, and everything had to change, our music included.

OPPOSITE PAGE:
When the Jackson 5 first came to California,
they all moved in with me.

Big changes were in the air, not only for the Supremes but also for Motown. After Cindy joined us and we were once again immersed in the excruciating demands of our career, Berry Gordy undertook the task of moving Motown to Los Angeles. I have no idea how long he worked up to this move, it must have been years. Can you imagine what it took to relocate such a complex, intricate operation two thousand miles away? Once again, Berry did it. He was certainly one of the smartest and most accomplished men I knew at that point in my life. Sometime around 1970, Motown, Berry, and I moved away from Detroit to start a new life in California. Mary and Cindy stayed behind because they didn't want to live in Los Angeles, and so the group dynamic became quite different. Instead of continuous rehearsals as we had before, we would get together to rehearse for specific tours and albums. I was just as glad because there was a great deal of internal jealousy then and the girls were really taking it out on me.

Berry loved living in California. He felt at home there almost immediately, and he seemed to thrive. It was a busy and lucrative place and time for him. This was when he officially signed the Jacksons to Motown. Through my relationship with Berry, I was able to meet Michael, a very special human being.

I have always known Michael to be a decent, sweet, and loving person who wants very much to make a difference in the world by helping others, especially children. He cares about animals and nature, and he believes that with a positive attitude, we can have whatever we want. He would like to produce and direct, and I believe he will have those opportunities. Whatever else he does, I hope he never stops making his beautiful music.

Michael was about eleven years old when we met. He was artistic, a quality that he and I shared. I remember that we used to go out to buy paints and easels and we did artwork together. He was always wonderful to have around. I am pleased that I touched him in the early days of his life, and I am sad that now I don't have the time to see him more often and to know him better. Careers have a way of separating people. Whether we are together or apart, my love for him never stops. It makes me happy that at one time we were close and that he cares for me. My love for him remains very dear, and our friendship will always be very important to me.

When the Jackson 5 first came to California, they all moved in with me. They have always been good to me. Despite the negative things that have been written about them, I knew them to be a unique family. People have picked them apart and gossiped about what they did or didn't do, but in my eyes Michael's mother is a very special and loving woman. The strength in those Jackson kids exists because of the strength and character of their father. Parenting is never easy. If you're too hard, you lose the kids; if you're too easy, you also lose them. Some fathers just have to be tough. Maybe if he hadn't been tough, the kids would never have arrived where they are today. Maybe the Jackson children will grow up to be very fine parents as a result of their own tough upbringing. I would like very much to see Michael settle down with a family of his own.

Apart from meeting the Jacksons, I was sort of lost in California, just trying to learn my way around a little bit. Although I had traveled extensively with the Supremes, I had never lived anywhere but Detroit. Los Angeles, the City of Angels, is so massive, so spread out. I had to rely on Berry most of the time. Of course that was how he liked it. My increased dependence on him only added to his ability to control and overpower me, which I allowed.

So there we were, Berry and I, not exactly living together, but in close proximity. I had rented a house just down the hill from him. We never talked about marriage, I wasn't ready for that. He is fifteen years older than I am, and he had already been married and had three kids. Although he had focused so much attention on me throughout my career, I had never felt that he was serious about me as a woman or a prospective wife. I wasn't really even his girlfriend, at least he never called me that, but he used whatever he could find to keep me under his wing.

Berry was a real ladies' man. He always had a lot of girlfriends hanging around; they knew he had the power to help them with their careers. Along with his personal magnetism there was something else about him that made him irresistible to women. Mary used to warn me about him, but I was too headstrong and wouldn't listen.

I remember him telling me that he didn't want his women performers to fall in love with anybody else or get married because it would ruin their careers. He felt that the husbands would try to be the boss and try to become too involved with their wives' work. And so that is why, when I met Bob Ellis Silberstein, I kept it to myself.

I met Bob in a men's clothing store on Santa Monica Boulevard. Just a regular day. I was on my way to the Beverly Hills Health Club when this store caught my eye. I needed a birthday gift for someone and went in to take a quick look before my workout. And there he was, looking really great, dressed in a white tennis outfit. "How attractive he looks," I thought.

"Are you a tennis pro?" I heard these words pop out of my mouth. I had been thinking about taking tennis lessons, but still it surprised me when I spoke up. I was sort of shy, and here I was, speaking to someone I didn't know. Unusual for me. Out of character. I wasn't flirting or trying to pick him up. Or was I? I don't think so.

"No, I'm not," he answered.

I smiled shyly and then, slightly embarrassed that I had opened the conversation and not knowing what to say next, I left the store and started across the street to the gym. The next thing I knew, he was standing beside me, helping me cross through the busy Santa Monica Boulevard traffic like a true gentleman. I was quite taken by him. He swung open the large glass door to the health club, and just as I was about to walk through, he stammered something.

"Would you . . . ? No, probably not," he said.

"What?" I encouraged him.

"I was wondering . . ." He stopped again.

"Wondering what?"

"No, that's all right. Forget it. Well, you probably wouldn't want to go to a movie, would you?"

"I might," I told him. That's it. "I'll be noncommittal," I thought to myself. "What's your name?" I asked him.

"Bob Silberstein."

In almost every photo session I tried to change my hair.

TOP LEFT: The first house I bought for my mother.
BOTTOM: Cindy, me, Mary, and Paul McCartney, a long long time ago.

OPPOSITE PAGE
TOP LEFT: I love these dresses. Funny, right?!
BOTTOM: This is how we used to rehearse–with the whole neighborhood. This must be at Florence's house.

ABOVE: A Bob Mackie special. I loved
wearing my hair pulled back.
OPPOSITE PAGE: The seventies was a decade of
experiments and extremes—
for the world and for me.

TV specials were a lot of fun then.

BELOW: This makeup was great. Can you tell it's me? Look—it's Ethel Waters and Bessie Smith.

Singing my heart out and happy.

"I'm Diana."

We exchanged phone numbers. I couldn't believe I was giving this stranger my number. Feeling like a nervous wreck, I immediately called my best girlfriend, Suzanne de Passe, from the changing room.

"I just gave my telephone number to a total stranger. I must be losing my mind, but he was really good-looking—wow!"

He called a few times, but because I wasn't home when he called, I avoided speaking to him. I think that some of the time we must have been on tour, anyway. I just wasn't sure that I should have given him my number. I was used to being under very tight security. Maybe my fear had something to do with it, too. But I was lonely. I had always been so protected when I traveled, I never got a chance to meet anyone unless they were in the shows with us. It seemed as if Mary used to meet a lot of great guys. I rationalized that working on my career was more important than dating and having fun.

When Bob kept calling, I finally spoke with him a few times, and then we started dating. We finally did go to the movies. Bob introduced me to a different side of life, one of adventure and play. I had been so overly protected in my career, and now here I was, flying down the street on the back of Bob's motorcycle, with the wind blowing through my hair, just as it did when I rode my bike as a child. And skiing, something that had been forbidden. After all, what if I broke my leg? A Supreme in a jeweled gown with a cast on her leg? Never! With Bob, I threw caution to the wind. I felt free and alive; I was sixteen years old again. He was wild and wonderful and so much fun. Tracee, our second daughter, is a lot like him, not so much in looks, but she acts like him, wild and funny. I remember when she was very young, she would get her silly thing going. She tickled me so much.

Laughter is important in my life, especially on tour. With all the work, Bob was a total change of pace. He has a wonderful sense of humor, and with him I laughed a lot. I think that was the best part of all. When things were good between us, I really enjoyed being married to him. He was an early riser, and he worked hard. These are qualities I really admire. And he loved to do things around the house. He was a good-looking man, and he loved good-looking cars and good-looking clothes. He wanted so much to be successful. He was a schoolteacher when I met him, and then he went on to become a manager in the entertainment business. We had a wonderful marriage for the first couple of years, but no matter how good things were, he felt he had to contend with the shadow of Berry Gordy.

I hadn't told Berry about Bob right away because even though Berry had plenty of other women, I knew he would discourage the relationship. It was something I was doing that he couldn't control and that would threaten him. Berry found out in his own way. When he learned that I was dating someone, he said he wanted to meet him. He treated it all quite innocently. It wasn't. Today, thinking back, he had his tactics. So, I introduced them, there was no longer any way of avoiding it. During the meeting, Berry was cordial and quite polite. Later, he had subtle ways of tearing Bob down. It was no surprise, but it was terribly uncomfortable, particularly because Berry's opinions mattered to me.

It seemed that the war was on. Berry and Motown showed up like jealous lovers. This may not be the way that it was, but it seemed that they didn't want me to be with anybody, and they kept making Bob wrong, showing me what he was not doing for me and not capable of giving me. Maybe Berry saw Bob as a threat and lashed out at him. It became a kind of tug-of-war. It was very demanding, and Bob got caught up in the competition. In the end, I guess Berry's fears were valid because Bob was very influential in helping me make my decision finally to leave Motown. He was always pointing out how, in many ways, Motown was taking advantage of me, keeping me off guard and frustrated all the time. We both understood that Berry was also trying to help me, but I had given him and Motown too much control. The tension between these two men in my life was high. I felt caught in the middle. I guess I admired Berry too much; I had him on a pedestal.

Bob and I certainly had our share of difficulties, and as time went on, things kept getting worse and worse. I remember one awful night when everything came to a head. Bob and I had been married for maybe six years; we already had the three girls. They were at home with a babysitter, and we were out riding in his jeep. I don't know what the fight was about, but Bob was so angry with me he started to speed and drive recklessly. I thought he was trying to kill me or kill us; he was that angry. It was as if he had lost his mind and was completely out of control. Certain that we were going to have an accident, I yelled at him to stop the car. He did, and I threw the door open and got out. I knew that I had to get away from him. When I saw what Bob was capable of, that he could be careless enough to endanger my life, his own life, and his children's future, I knew in that moment that our marriage was over. When I saw that a stupid argument was enough to allow Bob to lose control, I knew we were facing big problems.

Bob was not an abusive man, that was never his pattern. He was just going through tremendous problems. And I have learned, unfortunately the hard way, that I will not jeopardize my life and the safety of my family for anyone. This is what I have based many of my life-changing decisions on. Bob and I have remained friends. He was a good person then, and he is a good person now. He is the father of my children, and he and the girls are still close.

My decision to go out on my own began a long, tenuous road back to a different way of life, to a new city, to my film career, and eventually to higher love. When it began, I could not know what was in store. I only knew that I was afraid, and I had to turn to my faith to get me through.

> I love you Bob,
> I love you Berry,
> I love you Supremes,
> I love you Motown,
> and I cannot stay.

Days of Rage

Death, love, birth,
church
religions
fear
abuse
madness
black pride
loneliness, hurt, pain
murder

My career and adulthood blossomed during thirty revolutionary, exciting, violent, and daring years. While hope ran high and astronaut Neil Armstrong took his first step on the surface of the moon, this was also a frustrating era of rage. Our hearts ached with grief as the leaders whom we most admired and loved lost their lives to assassins' bullets.

In the dawning of the 1960s, newspapers and television were filled with warnings about a confusing place at the other end of the globe called Vietnam. My personal world was filled with long hours in recording studios, exhaustion from being on tour, and the normal challenges of growing up, both in my life and in my career. While I was singing "Stop! In the Name of Love" with the Supremes, our nation was plunging deeper and deeper into a war that many agreed our country never

OPPOSITE PAGE:
"If you can keep your head while all about you are losing theirs and blaming it on you . . ."–Rudyard Kipling

should have entered. So many kids rebelled by turning to drugs in order to escape a world that they thought was falling apart. Being in the music business, I was well aware of this growing drug scene that eventually claimed some of our most promising talents.

Fighting for equality in the sixties became a national movement. In my mind, it all began with four students staging a sit-in at a lunch counter in a five-and-dime store in Greensboro, North Carolina. Their courage started a chain reaction throughout the rest of the South over the next few years and even infiltrated into some of the Northern states.

In 1963, Dr. Martin Luther King touched our hearts and minds with his dream of hope. I had the opportunity to meet Dr. King once in Florida, where he was discussing fund-raising with Berry Gordy. I experienced him as a soft-spoken man with a beautiful spirit. His dream, one of inspiration, warmth, and hope, was dealt a blow a few months later when JFK died.

The day that President Kennedy was assassinated, I was back home in Detroit. I remember being in shock and watching the devastating event on television, over and over and over again. I heard the panic in the newscasters' voices. It was as if the whole world had gone crazy. Kennedy's assassination felt like an omen for the rest of the decade, and so it was. Martin Luther King was assassinated two years later, on April 4, 1968. Then, two months later, Robert F. Kennedy was killed while campaigning for the presidency.

I recall an uneasy stirring among women during this time. House-wives were no longer content to stand behind the stove and cook; they were moved and affected by the killings of our soldiers and our leaders. Women had become agitated. We had our own opinions. We began to speak out. All-male institutions like Yale started admitting women, and we began to break out into the workplace. Nineteen sixty-eight saw a real strengthening of the feminist movement, at the same time that blacks began to raise their fists in the Black Power salute.

Vietnam finally exploded, and I remember reading about the horrors of the My Lai Massacre. My life was touched personally by the war, as were the lives of so many others, because my brother Fred fought in

Vietnam. He had strong feelings about his family and his duty to his country. I remember how much confusion he had when he was over there. He wanted to believe in the American dream, he wanted to believe that he was doing the right thing for his country, but he could clearly see that the war was meaningless. Many of his friends were dying of drug addiction, either in Vietnam or when they came back, and he had lost faith in nearly everybody. It was a sad thing to see what was happening to him.

We used to send him letters and packages with little things that we knew he missed, like mustard and other items he couldn't get. He wrote us about how scared he was and how his friends kept dying over there. He was afraid of people he wasn't supposed to be afraid of, other Americans, especially some of the officers. He felt that he couldn't trust anyone.

Before he went to Southeast Asia, he had had all kinds of dreams. When he returned, they were gone. When Fred came back to us, he was very depressed and anxious. I remember when he was younger he had been wonderfully mechanical. He could take apart anything and put it back together again, even something as intricately mechanical as a clock. After his time in Vietnam, something changed and he no longer did that tinkering that he had loved so much. It took him a long time to resume living a real life. We all tried to be supportive of him, but in essence we knew that those years had robbed Fred of a good part of his life, as they did so many other young American men and women.

The tumultuous events of the sixties had an effect on my choices as a woman, as a human being, and as a professional. Women's liberation changed my way of thinking in every facet of my life, from how I handled my business affairs to my expectations in my personal life. The civil rights movement also had a profound effect on me. I was once invited to perform at Sun City, a segregated township in South Africa. They were willing to pay me large sums of money to perform there, but I declined. Arthur Ashe had told me about that place, that apartheid was active there, and along with many other empathetic performers, I took a stand. I refused to be exploited.

149

Much change had been initiated during the sixties, but there was still tremendous unrest. We had lost faith in the systems that we thought could protect us. When the decade ended, our youth was restless. No one knew what was next, but we were no longer willing to hide behind our dreams. As a nation, we were committed to speaking out and to looking at reality, no matter how harsh it might be. In my own life, change was also happening, and I was committed to letting it happen. I also had changed.

"Someday We'll Be Together"

January 14, 1970, Las Vegas, Nevada

Someday we'll be together.

The farewell performance of the Supremes at the Frontier Hotel. Everybody was there. I was waving good-bye to a dream. I never like to say good-bye. I'll see you soon, maybe. But never good-bye. Good-byes are too final.

That night in the dressing room, we tried to act as if this was just another show, as if things were okay, business as usual. But nothing was usual, and things were not okay. I stared at my face in the mirror, applying my makeup, fixing my hair, with a huge lump in my throat and a sting in my nose. I kept pushing the tears down, trying to swallow, holding on to myself so that I wouldn't break apart.

I stayed silent as I thought about what had happened to us. Saying good-bye to the Supremes was very difficult because I had worked so hard for the success of the group. I had made many personal sacrifices to promote the name, to keep the unity, to sing the songs, and to travel. Now, it was time to go. We just didn't fit anymore. It was like any other relationship or marriage. You put your time and energy into building something, and then, one day, you realize you have to walk away with nothing. I didn't take anything with me, not the gowns and costumes or

OPPOSITE PAGE:
I remember that first tour to Europe. Talk about culture shock! They didn't have any hamburgers there. They had something called a wimpy burger and it was wimpy. But they had fish and chips.

the name. I left all of that with Mary and Cindy for the forming of the new group. I had to take this risk.

The girls had treated me very badly. They had gone against me with a vengeance. They had blamed me, acted as if everything were my fault, that the press hadn't written about them, that Berry had chosen the songs that he wanted me to record. They were so blinded by jealousy that they never stopped to think that maybe, just maybe, my voice was better suited for the songs that Brian, Lamont, and Eddie wrote. That our records were selling because of my sound. It was inexplicable to me, but that's the way it was. I had been tormented, treated as if I were invisible, talked about behind my back when my back wasn't even turned. And yet I had tried to continue, I had tried to perform and pretend that all was well. When they finally became so angry that they stopped talking to me, it was too much to endure.

So I made a decision. I had been given the opportunity to do the film about Billie Holiday. At first we were considering that my leaving the Supremes would only be for a trial period. Then I thought more about it, and it didn't make sense, not for me or for them. The rehearsal period for the film was approaching. That would take a considerable amount of time because a great deal of dedication would be necessary on my part to understand the music and the complexities of the woman whom I was to play. Then the shooting would begin after that, and I was pregnant. That would force the girls not to work for much too long, not sing or make any money. It wasn't fair to them. The separation had to be permanent.

That night, as I prepared to perform with them for the last time, I knew that decision was one I would have to stay with. From this point on, there was no changing my mind. If things didn't turn out okay, I had to remember that it was my choice. I couldn't be like Florence, wanting back in when it was too late and blaming everyone else for her unhappiness. Things had gone too far. It had become impossible for me to record with them any longer. I was underweight and sickly because the negative energy had overwhelmed me. Most of the time I was too upset to eat. I stayed alone when we were on the road.

I guess some of this may be hard to comprehend from the outside. Our kind of life looks so glamorous and beautiful that everybody wants to do it. When the opportunity comes, it's different than you think. There's so much more to it than putting on a pretty gown, getting up onstage and singing. There is learning about the business itself, which cannot be overlooked or pushed to the side. And you have to be a quick study or someone will rip you off. You must know everything and keep your eye sharp, about contracts, deals, all of it. You must understand, I practiced all the time.

Throughout my career, my standards were high and I wanted to work with others who felt as I did. We had been pushed and pulled all over the place, we had suffered from the control. Leaving them was my statement that I was no longer willing to let anyone else define my life.

I think, even as I was putting on my costume to go out onstage for the last time, some part of me still didn't believe it was happening. But it was.

> This has been coming.
> Now it was here.
> Yes, I was leaving.
> When one door closes
> Another one opens.

In truth, it really hadn't happened soon enough. I had allowed myself to suffer too much while I kept trying to make things work. I guess I hadn't been completely ready yet. But I finally was ready. Ready to try something different, to give myself a new set of expectations about what I wanted in life, what would make me happy, how I wanted to behave. Ready to take responsibility for my own life, to be in charge of my own destiny. I had been living according to everybody else's rules for too long. I was ready to make my own decisions and my own choices.

A quiet sadness filled me as I realized that I was leaving, not only because I wanted to but also because I had to. They had hurt me very badly, beyond repair. We just weren't a group anymore. I knew this as I kept trying to look past the fears and the darkness to see the light. I needed to convince myself that this transformation was natural, it was what I wanted, and it was going to be all right.

Although I was fearful on the outside, deep within I knew I was okay. As a child, I always believed I had a guardian angel, and I prayed to her every night. She had been with me then, and she was still with me. I had been raised with a good sense of values. I had learned from everything, what my parents taught me, what happened in the streets, what I saw in my travels. Although I may not have fully understood this, I was already well equipped for the next phase. It was time to grow up. I had to. All I needed to do was trust myself. Trust. The ongoing theme in my life.

The curtain opens.

The show is supposed to be happy; we are singing our greatest hits. But I feel deeply sad. I step onstage. I am smiling and singing the words to the songs that everyone knows so well, the upbeat lyrics of my youth, but my heart is crying.

We close the evening with one of our most powerful songs. I never like to say good-bye.

Someday we'll be together.

I will always wonder if . . . ?

Where do I go?
Follow my heart.
Toward the future.

Clockwise from top: Berry, Diana, Mary,
and Florence.

Distance Traveled

Through the Blues

I left the Supremes in 1970. I think that at twenty-six I was old enough to know what I wanted and to make decisions based on what would make me happy in my life. When I first started singing, the thought of being an actress and making movies had never crossed my mind. My solo career began quite well, and I figured I would just keep on singing. After all, that's what I loved to do.

Starting a career on my own was not as difficult as people might think. Toward the end of my time with the Supremes, I had already been doing lots of performing without them and I had gone into the studio to record quite a few songs on my own. The technology of recording had begun to change, so everybody didn't have to sing at the same time. They would do tracks on the instruments first, then they would add the background singers, and finally they would put in the lead vocals. Once we had become Diana Ross and the Supremes, I was already separated, still a part of the group and, at the same time, not a part of the group.

I knew that the audience, the press, and the critics would be wondering how I was going to do as a soloist. The first time I walked out onstage alone, I said to the audience, "The name of this show is 'The

OPPOSITE PAGE:
Michele Comte takes very unique photos of me.

OVERLEAF:
For a public figure, enduring
unfounded criticism goes with the job.
I've learned not to be stopped by it.

Let's See If Diana Ross Can Do It By Herself Show.' " Immediately, there was big applause. I wanted them to get past their preconceived ideas right away. My fears had to do with whether the songs, the material, the show itself were good enough, so I worked very hard on the production and the presentation.

My first solo tour was a buildup to New York and Vegas. I played some small places out of town, just as you might try out a Broadway show. I wanted my shows to be very theatrical. Visuals have always been very important to me, and every day we would make notes and changes, as one would do in a big production. There were lots of light and sound cues, elaborate costumes and costume changes. In my shows, the musicians are not just a part of the background. They are an integral part of the show itself, and so is the lighting. All of these elements add to the overall drama.

Some performers stand onstage in one spot, sing their songs, and never talk to the audience. For me, bringing the audience in with me makes it more exciting as they become a part of the show. In a sense, the audience and I become one. I am not afraid of going into the audience. It makes me comfortable to be touched, to be able to touch them, and to see their faces and look into their eyes. It's like a conversation. That's the beauty of live shows. When I'm onstage, I talk about what I'm about to do, what the songs are about, and what they mean to me. Since the beginning of my career, this part of me has grown. I am so excited to be onstage and in the lights, communicating with an audience. The magic lifts me. I feel as if I am levitating, floating out into the room, close to the people. I feel that they can know me and that I can know them on a very human level.

As much as I love recording in the studio, there is nothing so magical as the energy onstage. I love working in the round, where the stage is in the middle and the audience surrounds me. They can see me from all sides, not just the front but also the back. The light surrounds me, too, and I can really see the faces. In this way, I feel closer to the people and there is a different freedom of movement. I can turn around, look up, and sit if I so desire.

I don't take my voice for granted. Singing has always been a natural gift for me. I try not to put too many restrictions on it. I simply trust in my talent and allow the feelings to come through my voice. I have no major techniques for my voice except to stay out of tension, to relax my vocal cords before going onstage by doing a little vocal exercising, and to breathe properly while I'm singing. I also try to stay in good physical shape. Traveling presents a great deal of stress due to jet lag and the changing of time zones. I reduce tension by only dealing with things that directly pertain to the performance. The only exception is that I am always on call for my family.

When I went out on my own, the stress of dealing with the group personality problems was immediately reduced. Today, I try to put together a band that consists of a group of individuals who have the same kind of integrity that I have about being on time, eating well, sleeping, and holding a serious commitment to the work. No drug or alcohol abuse. We have to work together as a unit, a team. We are like a family supporting each other, and if there is one bad apple who is causing problems and dissension, it ruins the group energy. Each person must take responsibility for the work that we're all doing. It isn't easy traveling together. We eat together, sleep together, fly together, and talk about our lives together. These relationships are very important, and there is a bonding that takes place. When one person gossips, I have to remove that stress as soon as possible. "One bad apple spoils the bunch." I have found this to be true, the hard way.

When I recorded my first solo song, "Reach Out and Touch (Somebody's Hand)," in April of 1970, it didn't do all that well in the beginning. It became a hit later on. I was determined to keep my career going. My solo act was moving along slowly. I was touring, performing, recording, and working very hard on my own. At the same time, I was preparing myself to play the role of Billie Holiday in *Lady Sings the Blues*. I had never gone to acting school, so the idea seemed very exciting. It was something new, challenging, different from anything I had ever done before. I had been singing and performing with the Supremes for ten years, and I was ready to do something completely different. This was it. It was a terrific challenge. And so, I was ready to take the next step.

When the announcement was made that I would be playing Billie Holiday, my mere acceptance of the role sparked a great deal of criticism. People said I didn't look like her, I didn't sing like her, I hadn't lived like her, and I hadn't experienced what she had. We hadn't even begun shooting and the press had already turned against me. I tried just to get past it and do the best I could in the role. After all, this was to be a movie, not a documentary.

For a public figure, enduring unfounded criticism is a necessary evil. As hard as it is to accept, I have learned not to be stopped by it. I guess, once again, I've learned the hard way because I've been criticized so much. My experience has taught me not to personalize what I read in the press, that, ultimately, it's only a part of the music or a scene in a film that people are finding fault with, not me as a human being. I do feel that some forms of criticism are necessary and growth-producing, especially when they come from people who know something and want to help. I am grateful for constructive criticism, and I listen well, hoping I can improve what I am doing. When criticism focuses on how you look, being too old, too young, I try not to pay any attention. I have no interest in what people have to say when they are being hateful, negative, or just plain mean.

It was especially difficult to ignore the criticism in this case because it tapped into my own deepest fears. Since I had no previous acting experience, this was a process of blind trust, of real effort, of believing in myself, trusting my instincts, and taking a leap of faith. I would have to jump right in and go for it and block out all the rest. I remember speaking with an acting coach at the very beginning of our rehearsal period and confiding in him, "I've got to do this film, and I don't know the first thing." I'll never forget what he said to me; it made all the difference: "You'll do fine. Just don't be afraid to make mistakes and trust yourself. There's no wrong way to act. Be real and honest, and above all, don't be afraid to make a fool of yourself."

This was the most important advice anyone could ever give me because the role was extraordinarily demanding in so many ways. In order to play this part, I was literally up against the wall to dissolve all the images that everybody had about me. I found out that if I was afraid to look stupid, I would never learn anything, so I had to close my eyes and just do it.

Berry really believed that I could be a great actress. He demonstrated an undying faith in me. I've always said if one person believes in me, I will try to move mountains. I have fought really hard to do what he believed I could do. I have been fortunate in my life. In my youth, my mother took this supportive role of believing in me unconditionally, and then it was my elementary school teacher, Miss Page. Later Berry took over. With that kind of support, I think we can do anything. As Berry believed in me, he also believed in himself. We were a team. As he encouraged me to step out as an actress, he was creating himself as a successful producer. I was the vehicle he was using to create his own dreams. For whatever reasons we believed in each other, the end result is the same: He helped me grow and expand my horizons in a larger dream than I even had for myself.

165

How Berry knew that I could be a dramatic actress, I cannot say. The only acting I had done was with the Supremes when, in the early days, we had done some pieces with George Schlatter for television specials. That work had all been light comedy, and the sketches were pretty silly. I had never done anything dramatic, not even a reading. I guess Berry had noticed the energy I projected on TV, and because he knew me and how hard I was willing to work, he had the courage to support me. With that degree of encouragement, I made a commitment to move past my fears and doubts.

When I made the decision to do the movie, I had just become pregnant with my first baby, Rhonda. I had always wanted to be a mother, and I remember thinking, "I can't do this film because I'm going to have a baby." The film kept getting delayed, as they often do, and I used my nine months of pregnancy to read whatever I could about Billie Holiday, about drugs, and about drug addiction. I studied everything related to the film that I could get my hands on. This was a perfect time for research. I also spent time recording. During each of my pregnancies, I have worked through my sixth month. I really never stop.

As often happens with first pregnancies, I was sick a lot, and I didn't go out very much. I took this further opportunity to study, read, and listen to Billie Holiday's music. What I mostly heard was a tremendous pain coming from deep inside of this talented woman, but I don't think that the pain was a part of her natural being. I think the pain came from her drug addiction because it was absent from her earliest performances, the ones she did before she became drug-addicted. When the pain was not present, what was left was a very interesting and unique sound. Even when she was older and her voice had begun crackling, if you listened carefully beyond the crackling and the pain, that incredible sound was still there.

During my nine months of intense research, I made some important decisions about how I would interpret the role, one of them being that I would not try to sound like Billie. That felt like the wrong approach. My voice is so different from hers. I would work to bring through my own sound. Strangely, since I listened to almost nothing else during that time, I took on the same phrasing she used, and in this way I ended up sounding a lot like her after all.

Sometimes I would stand up and look at myself in the mirror, just as I did as a child when I was trying to be Etta James, and I would study my face while I thought about Billie, asking questions. What did she think about herself? What did she feel when she sang? This was my research, this was my personal form of acting classes. I spent all of my time with her, her music, and also photographs of her that people sent me and that Berry was able to obtain from her personal files.

Right after I had my baby, and just before we began the actual filming of the project, we recorded the songs. I had already been work-ing with the script, or at least an early version of it, so I could see where in the unfolding story each song would be placed. That was a great help to me because I could determine whether she was going on drugs, all the way addicted, coming off, or drug-free during each particular song. Her relationship with drugs at each specific phase in her life created a difference in how the song was to be interpreted, musically and emotionally. Was she clear, was she stoned, was she focused, what was happening in her life then? These questions always had to be taken into consideration when I made my expressive and artistic choices. Then, once I had integrated that information in my head, I could forget about it and just let the song happen. I ended up doing the same thing with the acting scenes when we started filming.

Besides the material that had been expressly written for the Supremes, I had also sung standards with them, but never this bluesy, low-down kind of stuff. I was not a stranger to it. I always loved jazz, and throughout my childhood, I had been influenced by the music of the old jazz greats like Ethel Waters, Bessie Smith, Ella Fitzgerald, and of course Billie Holiday. The word "jazz" suggests action to me, and I feel dignity in it. This is the same dignity that originates in my black heritage, the dignity that was always so obvious in the souls of my parents.

I like to think that the dignity and pride that my mother and father expressed, even when they were financially hard-pressed, is something that they have passed on to me. I have always cried easily, and these deep feelings come pouring out of my music. My mother always felt that the depth of feeling expressed in my music went way beyond my personal experience. She used to call me "an old soul," and I liked that.

The lyrics in jazz and blues are often about mourning and "losing my man," but I still see the validity in these kinds of songs. Loss and sorrow are a part of all of our lives. Although I like to sing positive songs, words and sounds that inspire people to feel good, we need to hear about all sides of life. For me, jazz means freedom. It is about breathing, and a certain relaxation is present in the music. Improvisation is often a large part of singing jazz, but I like to keep that in its proper place. If improvisation is a natural part of the freedom, not just a gimmick to make a point, only then will I improvise.

As I began to do Billie Holiday's music, it was a brand-new style for me, at times slightly intimidating but mostly exciting. What was most important then, and continues to be with any kind of music I'm doing, is that I need to find identification for myself with each song, something

that makes the song come alive in my own experience. People may have
wondered how I could have identified with the depth and feeling of a
Billie Holiday, our lives had been so different, but I was a woman, too.
There had been miseries and disappointments in my own world. When I
was singing things like "My Man" or "Lover Man," instead of trying to
relate to her life, I would think about the sadness or loneliness in my
own love affairs. I may not have had Billie Holiday's unique set of
problems, but I had lived, I had my own experience to draw from, I had
been hurt in my own life.

When the shooting began, I had to dig down deep inside myself to do
the actual acting. I don't know where my knowledge came from. Again,
I think it was about trusting the people who were trusting me. Sidney J.
Furie, the director, was a great source of strength for me and, of course,
Berry. He used to coach me and tell me, "Now forget everything I told
you and go out there and have a good time." He obviously knew I
wasn't going to forget what he had told me. He was encouraging me to
integrate the techniques for my acting as I did for my singing. Once
Furie and Berry had directed me to the point where they could trust me,
they let me go and left me to my own devices. If I felt that a certain scene
required laughter or tears, they let me improvise. Berry would say, "It's
only a film. Do anything you want." So all I needed to do before I got to
the set was memorize the lines and then let the moment be real. I would
feel that I was in that actual room and whatever we were doing in the
film was really happening. Acting is a wonderful thing; it gives you the
opportunity to draw on your own moments. Since I had been performing onstage for many years, I already had experience in doing this.
When you sing a sad song, you must become sad and you must find
something inside yourself to create that. Berry knew that I had the
ability to act because he had seen me find such deep emotions inside
myself when I performed.

During the tedious filming process, I learned to tolerate the endless
retakes by using them to my advantage. After each take, I would say to
myself, "I'll do it better next time. It can only get better, not worse. If I
get to do it one hundred times, I'll just keep trying to do it different and

better and see what comes up." So next time, I'd take a completely different point of view and give them a completely different reading.

I was basically treated with a great deal of respect and trust by the people involved in the making of the film. I was pleased that they let me watch the dailies, the footage that was shot the day before, as this helped me see how I was doing and I felt good about how things were progressing. But it was a very hard time. I had to throw myself into Billie Holiday's life, and her existence was riddled with pain and suffering. I was given my own space on the Paramount lot where we were shooting. I re-created Billie's original bedroom, her house, her dressing room. I had some of her actual things in these rooms, and I would go there before six o'clock every morning. There I would be, in Billie Holiday's life, until I left at night. Besides the weekends and my wonderful lunchtimes when they would bring my baby to me, I was completely immersed in the life and the psyche of Billie Holiday.

Shelly Berger, my manager, would pick me up every morning, and we would run through my lines in the car on the way to the lot. We would also run through them briefly each night after the shoot. Since Shelly was acting as my private coach, he used to memorize the lines right along with me. He was my best coach and a good friend, and he stayed on as my manager for many years. Shelly supported me beautifully and spent a great deal of time with me. He was the only person I can remember who could sit through an entire recording session until we were finished. It took stamina and dedication for that; the sessions would often run well into the wee hours of the morning. So it was hard for the people who were sitting there listening. Shelly would always stay right up to the end, taking care of me, making sure I had coffee or something to eat. He showed up in the same way for *Lady Sings the Blues*. Trust and support have always been the key for me. When these qualities are present, I have been able to accomplish my greatest feats.

In a very short period of time, I lived Billie Holiday's toughest moments of a very tough life. Maybe I didn't live them exactly as she did because I never did drugs, but I vicariously learned some of her hardest lessons, and these lessons have become a part of the fabric of my own life. Things like the price you pay for being out of control in love, for being overly vulnerable when it isn't safe, both in life and in business. And you learn caution against susceptibility to drugs. That's about the addiction to the highs. It's about being onstage when the highs are so high: the lights, the applause, the adoration. Then the performance is over and you go home or you're on the road and you're all alone in a strange hotel room somewhere. You want to escape that, you want the lights, the power, the energy. You want to keep the high, to stay in that exalted moment, to be excited all the time. But that can't be.

What we really need in life is balance. Not too low, not too high, just somehow to stay easy in the middle. There's a balanced way to sleep, to eat, even to drink. To upset the balance is to get offtrack. And it's dangerous. For me, my kids have always helped me keep my sense of balance. When they cry for Mom, I don't have time to be Diana Ross. For example, both of my little boys had nightmares last night. When they cried for me, I had to be there. So I was up all night. They didn't care that I had meetings or that I wanted to write today. They just needed their mother. They keep me on purpose by reminding me what my real purpose is. Maybe if Billie Holiday had had kids, she wouldn't have done drugs. The greatest gift that my kids give me is the reminder that I'm not so great. I'm just ordinary.

Finally, what I received from playing Billie Holiday is a richer part of myself. The music was so rich with emotion and feeling. I liked the places within myself to which I needed to go to perform the songs. So I started selecting songs for my own performances that would pull more from me in a much deeper place. I was able to use my work as therapy, as I did a few years later when I filmed *The Wiz*. I seem always to be able to use my work that way, especially when I am performing. I can sing it out really loud, from my toes to the top of my head, and then I can just get over whatever is bothering me. Whenever I use my music that way, I like to think of that great moment in *Moonstruck* when Cher's character slaps her boyfriend's face and says, "Snap out of it!" When I'm really belting out a song, it's as if I'm doing that to myself.

I had the great honor of being nominated for an Academy Award for my role in *Lady Sings the Blues*. It was doubly exciting because it was my first acting endeavor. Although I didn't win, it didn't matter. I was thrilled to have been given the opportunity to pay tribute to such an exceptional black woman and such a wonderful singer. Billie Holiday still haunts me, and it was a win to have made the music at all. Ultimately, that movie brought me a multitude of gifts, among them the rush of having taken on a powerful challenge and doing well, a new-found sense of myself, the realization that anything is possible, and the courage and conviction to keep moving forward in my life.

Ross Goods

*Success is nothing if you don't have
someone to share it with.*

I continued to do concerts and to release albums between my films. Then *Mahogany* was released by Paramount Pictures in 1975. I really enjoyed doing that movie because it was all about fashion. I love clothes, everyone knows that, and with *Mahogany* I was given the opportunity to design all the clothes and wardrobe for Tracy Chambers, the character I played.

Although singing was always there for me, I also had a great interest in design. The high school I attended, Cass Tech, accepted kids from all over the city, but you had to have a certain grade average to be accepted. Cass had an extensive curriculum to prepare people for many different fields. It had especially good chemistry and biology departments for teenagers, like my sister Bobbi, who wanted to be doctors. If you wished to major in business, you could go across the street to Commerce, take typing and shorthand, and still be preparing for college. Cass was a college prep school.

I was attracted to the school because of the design department. I studied fashion design and costume illustration, and then I took cosmetology classes in the evenings. There were so many different things that interested me. I wanted to be a model. I wanted to be a fashion designer.

OPPOSITE PAGE:
Designing, clothing, and fashion are very important aspects of who I am.

I had always loved pulling things together. My family didn't have a great deal of money to spend on clothes, so I would design fashions for myself from old clothing. I would remake hand-me-downs. Mama was a self-taught seamstress, and she taught me that if the fabric is good, you can restyle anything. We sometimes would buy inexpensive fabrics, and then we'd make up something really special, one of a kind. I was voted the best-dressed girl in my graduating class, which made me feel good about my sense of style.

The part of Tracy was specially written for me. I was excited about having Tony Richardson as director. He had done some really great movies and won an Academy Award for *Tom Jones*. I learned a lot from Tony. We had a terrific working relationship. For example, I would go on the set of Tracy's apartment and fix it the way in which I thought she would live. I had created a background for Tracy—where she put her family pictures, where she put her sewing machine. Tony and I discussed all the camera shots. First thing in the morning, we would go to location and he would have me set the room up the way I was most comfortable. Then I would go to my trailer for makeup and hair and he would light the set, based on what I had walked through.

The film was shot in Chicago and then in Rome. I loved living in Italy for the production. It was beautiful, and the food was really great. I had my own private villa with two lovely people to take care of me. I was able to take the children, Rhonda and Tracee, and being able to have them with me made it even more special.

Billy Dee Williams also starred in the film. There was always good chemistry going on between us. I really love working with talented people. I learn a lot from them. Billy Dee is like family to me. Since *Lady Sings the Blues*, there is this wonderful closeness. He's very playful, and we tease each other a lot in a romantic sort of way. But we've never had any relationship other than working together and being pals.

Tony Perkins was the other lead. He was a deep man, and he had this very special mystery about him. We enjoyed working together very much. During this last year, I was so sad to hear that he had died of AIDS. We have lost so many creative and talented people to AIDS, many of them designers and people in the fashion industry. It was in 1981 when I first heard about someone I knew getting AIDS. It was a friend of mine, a beautiful young man who was a model in New York.

That was years ago. Today, the numbers have reached the hundred thousands and there is still a great deal of ignorance about this devastating disease. It seems to me that the younger generation is filled with confusion. They have very little understanding about the illness, and as a result they view sexuality and their human needs with fear. Many of my fans, people who have followed me for years, have died of AIDS. This has affected me deeply, and I want to be supportive in heightening AIDS awareness. Education is most important. As parents, we must not be afraid to talk openly to our children about sexuality. I feel it is our responsibility to teach our young people how to take care of themselves sexually. They must know that if they don't, the consequences are serious and they could die.

Mahogany was my debut in the fashion business. Paramount gave me an entire floor to use when I went about making my patterns. In the final fashion scene, I wanted to make all of the costumes in a Kabuki-like style, only more surrealistic. Since I had learned about fabrics, sewing, millinery, wardrobe, knitting, and crocheting at Cass Tech, designing the costumes was a dream come true.

The first thing I did was put together a studio. I hired sketch artists, and I went through the script, marking where Tracy needed special clothes and exactly what she needed to wear. The whole process was exciting, plus the story was one with which many young women can identify: going into the fashion business and understanding the rejection that often goes along with being a designer.

Midway through the movie, Berry replaced Tony as director. It was a mutual parting of the ways. There was a creative battle going on. Berry wasn't happy with what he saw in the rushes or with the dialogue. When Berry took over, the project became a different project from the one I had been working on. There was tension and stress, but I was still learning from everyone. Again, I was allowed to view all the dailies and contribute my creative input.

Overall, I was pleased with *Mahogany*, and since the release of the movie, I have received mail from many youngsters who want to be fashion designers. In terms of box office, *Mahogany* didn't do very well. For me, success comes in many different forms. It's not always box-office receipts. Having good working relationships, learning about film, and being able to develop my design talents made the movie successful for me.

Clothes often have reflected my many moods, and there are designers who can touch me with their whimsy. I am very playful, so I like to have really fun, trendy clothes such as jeans or leather pants, shorts or T-shirts, boots or big old things with holes in them. The glamorous gowns are for the stage, but my fun clothes are for every day.

Then there are clothes I wear as a businesswoman—suits, nice dresses. I like Calvin Klein very much, also Anne Klein. I like Ralph Lauren for certain occasions and Thierry Mugler for spicy evenings out. For some of the TV shows I have done, I've worn a spectacular draped outfit by Thierry rather than a beaded gown. I think he's a magnificent sculptor, and some of his outfits truly are works of art.

There are so many designers I admire, especially those who work with me on my stage costumes. I have worked with Elizabeth Courtney's Ray Aghayan and Bob Mackie since the early days, and together we have designed some fabulous costumes. They are one-of-a-kind outfits, and I've kept most of them, intending one day to make an exhibit.

Designing, clothing, and fashion are a very important part of who I am. While I was living in New York in the 1980s, I had an opportunity to design a line of clothing for Simplicity Patterns. That was really a lot of fun for me. I even had my own line of Diana Ross panty hose. I wanted to design a stocking that didn't have any lines and was smooth all the way to the waistline. I remember the people I was dealing with at that time thought the line could never be done, that the hose wouldn't be strong and would split. Years later, once my line was discontinued, someone else came out with the same concept.

One day I would like to design a line of lingerie, and I am very excited about creating children's clothes. So designing is still very much a part of who I am, and *Mahogany* is still very much a part of my life. For me, it was definitely a winner.

Learning to Fly

When I think of home, I think of a place
Where there's love overflowing.
I wish I was home, I wish I was back there
With the things I've been knowing.

Wind that makes the tall trees bend into leaning,
Suddenly the raindrops that fall have a meaning.
Sprinkling the scene.
Makes it all clean.

This song in *The Wiz* entitled "Home" always makes me feel good because it brings me back to my beginnings. It's a song that reminds me never to lose myself in the brilliance of the lights. It returns me to my roots. In the summer of 1977, when I was first beginning rehearsals for the part of Dorothy in *The Wiz*, I felt lost. I was no longer certain where to be. I had left Detroit for L.A. and L.A. for New York, trying to find my place.

I asked myself over and over again, "Where is my home?" Detroit, where I knew the surroundings, where I had family? It had certainly felt like home, there had been love overflowing. But I didn't live there anymore. I hadn't lived there for quite some time. Was the Motown family home? It had been my creative center for seventeen years, a place where I was nurtured, where I had worked hard and long. Even when things were difficult, I knew I had a special place there.

OPPOSITE PAGE:
On my own in New York, I was determined to start fresh, not holding on to any unhappiness or anger.

What about the home life I had built in L.A. with Bob? That had felt like home, especially since it was where my children had been born. I had a lovely home there, but something had changed. Bob and I weren't the same. It didn't feel right anymore. We had grown in different ways.

We had tried to mend the marriage, but we were having so many problems. He knew I loved him, or at least I thought he did. Whether he knew it or not, Bob was in a great deal of pain. The pressure of his trying to overcome Berry Gordy's importance in my life was too much. Berry was too demanding; I was too confused. It was a messy triangle, and I found it too complicated. I knew it; I saw it coming, but I was powerless at that time to do anything about it. I wished he had been stronger so that instead of becoming twisted up in the confusion he could have freed himself. We had gotten caught up in a sticky web. I tried to keep myself balanced in the desperate tug-of-war between the two of them with me in the center. I couldn't. I felt torn apart all the time, not happy with Bob, not happy with Berry, not happy at Motown. It was a painful time for me. I tried kidding myself that I could find a way to make it all work, but I knew that I would eventually have to leave them both if I wanted to find peace. I would have to change everything, to start over, to wash it all away,

Sprinkling the scene,
Makes it all clean.

I tried coming to New York to be away from it all. I really did still love Bob, and I thought that time apart might save us, give us time to think and give him a chance to sort out some things. I felt disoriented; it surely would have been nice to have been back home again. Home with Bob, with my kids, my loving family. I hoped that there was a chance, that the separation might be the answer.

Maybe there's a chance for me to go back
Now that I have some direction.
It sure would be nice to be back home
Where there's love and affection.

And just maybe I can convince time to slow up,
Giving me enough time in my life to grow up.
Time, be my friend,
Let me start again.

But that didn't happen. We couldn't start again. It's not that we didn't try. We did. Bob came to meet me in New York to talk things over. We tried to get back together again. It just didn't work. Too much had happened that had damaged our connection, and we didn't know how to help each other. I guess we were just too young; both of us were still growing up. I had to face the truth that it was over. I finally flew to California to get my divorce, and when I returned I knew that I was on my own.

Questions. Was this a temporary move? Would I be returning to Detroit? Or would I be staying in New York or some nearby suburb? I didn't have any real friends in this crowded city, just a few scattered social acquaintances. Everything had changed so much recently, nothing was the same. What did I have to go back to? I was afraid, but somewhere deep down inside, I knew that everything would be all right. I had to just keep going and blindly trust, one day at a time.

Suddenly my world's gone and changed its face.
But I still know where I'm going.
I have had my mind spun around in space,
And yet I've watched it growing.

If you're listening, God, please don't make it hard to know
If we should believe the things that we see.
Tell us, should we run away, should we try and stay,
Or would it be better just to let things be?

I felt just like Dorothy, lost in some faraway land, trying to live in the "I don't know what's next," trying to trust that I would be fine. I kept my house in Los Angeles, but I rented a friend's apartment in Manhattan until I decided if I was going to look for something more permanent. At least my children were with me, and that kept my mind off myself. I

enrolled them in school for September. That was when we were scheduled to start shooting. My mom came to give me a hand with the girls
and to help me start organizing my life, which included my financial
affairs, something I hadn't taken the time to understand. I had left a lot
of that to Berry and Motown, and that was part of the problem with Bob,
who had explained how stupid that was.

This was one more area I had to change, one more thing I had to learn
from scratch. I was determined to do it clean, to start fresh without the
old pain, not holding on to any unhappiness or anger.

And so I looked around and here I was, on my own in New York,
overwhelmed with the newness of it all. Was this home, this big city
with so much noise and commotion? It was not a place I really knew. It
felt so impersonal. How could I ever call it home? And yet, somehow, I
knew that it was up to me, that I needed to make it real, that I needed to
create it here for myself and my girls. This was to be my initiation into
taking responsibility for myself. I quickly learned that I was doing the
right film; Dorothy and I were obviously asking the same questions. I
hoped we would find the same answers.

I decided to stay because Rhonda, Tracee, and Chudney were getting
settled into school and they liked their new friends. They helped me
make that hard decision.

Living here in this brand-new world might be a fantasy,
But it's taught me to love, so it's real to me.
And I've learned that we must look inside our hearts
To find a world full of love like yours, like mine.
Like home.

A Strange Wind

How am I knowing which way to go,
Not knowing which, where, I'm coming from.
What is this feeling?
Where is this feeling?
When does a feeling show?

I'm not sure that I'm aware
If I'm up or down,
If I'm here or there,
I need both feet on the ground.

The first thing I did when I arrived in New York was what I always do when I am about to embark upon a new project. Research. This is how I begin to get involved in a role, how I help myself feel that I have both feet on the ground. I like to find out everything I can about my new character and the world she inhabits so that I will deeply understand not only her words and actions in the film itself but also where she has been, where she is going, and the inner motivations and desires that drive her. I must completely immerse myself in the character in order to feel truly at home in her skin. There's that word again, home. Now that I had left Detroit, along with my quest for the inner workings of Dorothy I was looking for the same things about myself.

As I dived headlong into my new film project, I began to realize an incredible connection between my life and Dorothy's. The sheltered

OPPOSITE PAGE:
Both Dorothy in *The Wiz* and I suddenly found ourselves in a strange land where nothing was familiar.

girl who suddenly finds herself in a strange land without any of her old friends. All new frames of reference. Nothing familiar. And her task is to find her way home. Both physically and metaphorically. This role was to be a great gift to me, as it so closely resembled the role I was living in my life at that time. My search for the inner workings of Dorothy's being, for the answers to her deepest questions, was truly the search for my own questions and longings. They were one and the same.

As I arrived in New York, I went to see *The Wiz*, which was playing on Broadway. Although this was the version after which our film adaptation was modeled, it turned out that many things were different. As my research progressed, I was surprised to discover that many "Oz" renditions had been created and performed over the years, the most popular and well-known being, of course, *The Wizard of Oz*, the magical classic starring Judy Garland. There had also been other wonderful versions, all quite varied, each with its own unique look, costuming, and script. Although they were decidedly different interpretations, the theme was always the same: the overcoming of fear and obstacles, the return to innocence in the ultimate search for self.

Why do I feel like I'm drowning,
When there is plenty of air?
Why do I feel like frowning?
I think the feeling is fear.

Maybe I'm just going crazy,
Letting myself get uptight.
I'm acting just like a baby,
But I'm gonna be all right.

Somewhere deep down inside, Dorothy always knew that she would prevail, and in my new life, so did I. It was about trusting in something you couldn't see, at times a difficult mission. Starting right from the beginning, there was a lot of help and guidance along the way. While pouring through the vast "Oz" material that I had gathered for my research, I discovered a great gift. It was an annotated version of

L. Frank Baum's *Wizard of Oz*. During my study of this book, some of
the previously disjointed pieces started fitting together. I began clearly
to see the possibility that everything occurring in Dorothy's dream was
a direct reflection of her life, her pain that was crying out for attention,
the unresolved areas that she needed to learn to define, to handle, to care
for, to work on so that she might grow and be fulfilled as a whole person.
And once again, I saw that the process was the same for me.

Although I had already been aware of the implications of the message
of *The Wiz*, it suddenly took shape and form as never before. As the
function of each of the characters became obvious, as I could see that
they spelled out a different aspect of Dorothy's essence, the story came
together, each piece neatly fitting into the whole. It was a joy to fit it
altogether, the kind of satisfaction you feel as you put in place the last
pieces of a giant jigsaw puzzle.

The Scarecrow was a representation of Dorothy's hunger for knowledge, the part of her that longed to know more about life and living. So
fitting that he should be the first character she came upon in her dream,
the first new friend that she made. The Tinman personified Dorothy's
craving for love, the search for her heart, the deep need in her (in all of
us, for that matter) to increase her capacity to give and to receive love.
And the Lion, the supposedly mean old lion, was yet another part of
Dorothy's psyche. His loud and aggressive roars, designed to distance
people by projecting fear and anger into their hearts, were merely a
cover-up of his own fears and rage, an armoring to protect the sweetness
and vulnerability of his, and of course Dorothy's, gentle heart. Finally,
there was the Good Witch, Dorothy's protector, the subconscious part
of her that saw through the illusion of separateness, that already knew
the answers, and that was always there to show her the way.

For me, the songs themselves held the most importance. They were
written by Charlie Smalls, and along with the beauty of his music, his
lyrics were uncanny. They so perfectly related to what was going on
inside of me: my fear of showing my true feelings, the confusion of
being in a new and unfamiliar place, the isolation of being alone, having
no friends, trying to find my way one step at a time. It was all there, in

the words to those wonderful songs, and I got to voice them each time I
opened up my mouth to sing:

> *Here I am in a different place,*
> *In a different time*
> *In this time and space.*
> *I don't wanna be here.*
>
> *In a different place,*
> *In a different time,*
> *Different people around me.*
> *Alone.*
> *I don't know where I'm going.*
> *I'm here on my own,*
> *And it's not a game.*
> *A strange wind is blowing.*

And so, as I blew into the strange new world of New York, my life
was full and busy. I was occupied with two major tasks: setting up a
comfortable place to live for my girls and me and the research on my
character. Fortunately, both of these took off quite well. My kids began
to attend their new school, and almost immediately I saw incredible
progress in them. I think it was due to the fact that they were feeling
more secure and had more of me than they had had in California. That
was important for them and for me, too. In truth, we all needed each
other. The Manhattan apartment that Rhonda, Tracee, Chudney, and I
were staying in was very small, especially compared to my house in
Beverly Hills. And yet it worked to our advantage, proving to be
exactly what we most needed. We were able to live more privately
because we didn't need a large staff to take care of things as we had in Los
Angeles. So a bonding took place between my girls and me that I do not
think would have otherwise been possible. They always knew where I
was, and they always knew that when they came home from school, I
would be there for them. That gave them the security they needed to
make a healthy transition. Once I felt they had what they needed, I was

free to concentrate on my own needs. As I immersed myself in this new and exciting project, a lot of healing was taking place. I was settling into my new life, healing from my divorce, dropping my dependency on Berry, cutting my ties to Motown, and immersing myself in this new and exciting project.

The film proved to be tremendously therapeutic for me, a strong vehicle in which to find myself. I don't think I was completely aware at the time of how perfectly Dorothy's life reflected my own, how powerfully the film was demonstrating my personal search for self. I was somewhat aware of this, but I was inside of it, just doing it. As things often go, the depth of the immensity of the experience did not fully hit me until I viewed it in hindsight, though I always identified with the beautiful and insightful songs. I had great joy in performing them and felt that I was taking in and putting out an important, positive, meaningful message.

The script was brilliantly written by Joel Schumacher, a longtime friend. Joel and I were aligned in our beliefs, so we identified with the project in a big way. We were personally driven by the underlying theme of the film: the relentless and sometimes lonely search for self, the overcoming of all obstacles in the desire to become centered and comfortable in one's own skin, the driving quest for the knowledge that we are on the path back home.

My first meeting on the film was with the director, Sidney Lumet. Costume designer Tony Walton and Joel were also there, and the production office was literally sizzling with energy. It was an exciting meeting. They showed me some of the costumes that were in progress and how they visualized the look of the various characters. It was at this meeting that they told me they were considering Michael Jackson for the role of the Scarecrow, Dorothy's first friend along the path, who is looking for his brain, or deeper knowledge. I was enthusiastic. I thought it would be wonderful for Michael and me to work together. Michael and I were in pretty close contact during that time. We spoke on the phone every couple of days and usually saw each other about once a week, when our careers permitted. Even though this would be Michael's very first acting role, I told them that I considered him an ideal choice.

His personality suited the role, he was a superb dancer and there was a great deal of dancing designed for this lavish musical production, and we were already very close friends.

We began our rehearsals by reading the script straight every day. At first, it was just Sidney and I reading it together. Then we would bring in one character at a time. They had definitely decided to go with Michael, so Sidney, Michael, and I would do the next readings. And then it was Michael, Sidney, Nipsey Russell, who played the Tinman, and I. And on and on until we had the entire cast there. Each time, we would read the whole script from beginning to end. I found it to be too much rehearsal. Not that it was too much work but rather that the material became overrehearsed. Of course this is a personal preference, but I feel that endless reading of a script often results in a loss of spontaneity. In the case of *The Wiz*, it is my opinion that some of the magic that is so necessary to pull off such a story was sacrificed in the name of preparedness. But I was a part of a team and I didn't want to create problems, so I did it their way.

Even before the actual shooting began, we were working very hard. The rehearsal time was grueling for all of us. We would spend the mornings reading the script over and over, and once we had finished, we would move on to the dance rehearsals. *The Wiz*, being a lavish musical production, had a huge ensemble with superb but complicated choreography. The first part of the afternoon was dedicated to the individual dance numbers like "Ease on Down the Road," with Michael, Nipsey, Ted Ross as the Cowardly Lion, and me. Then later, the entire troupe would join us for the group numbers. Although I was in very good physical shape, the choreography was challenging. There was a great deal of fast running. Although it may have appeared simple, the set design was immense and complex, and that continuous high-speed movement through the maze of sets was sometimes physically dangerous.

The heels on my shoes were not very high, but they were high heels nonetheless. If you've done any kind of running at all, you know how hard it can be on the legs, even in proper running shoes. I had to dash at high speeds, skip, dance, and jump up and down on tables in high heels.

When you rehearse a film and during the shooting, you repeat things over and over again. It was no surprise that I began having problems with my knees. But I pressed on, dealing with whatever arose. Of course the director pushed us all. I was so accustomed to doing more than anybody else I always did whatever was expected of me and just a little bit more.

As we moved closer to the time when the actual shooting would begin, I was still feeling like a stranger in my own life. I still had a lot of personal work to do, but as September approached, I was healing from some difficult years, feeling more hopeful, and I was ready to face whatever came next.

Hello, World

If you believe,
In your heart you'll know,
No one can change
The path that you must go.

Believe what you feel,
Believe there's a reason to be.
Believe you can make time stand still,
If you believe in yourself.

Even though *The Wiz* was disappointing at the box office, it was a huge success in my life and in the lives of many of the other people involved. Making the movie when I did helped me work through a lot of difficult times and make many important decisions. I had to straighten out my life, to figure out things that were new and confusing. I had never taken control of my own world before, and there were many puzzles I had to unravel that I didn't know anything about. I felt blind in many arenas, but circumstances were forcing me to rise to the occasion. I had to feel my way through. In the meantime, shooting on *The Wiz* swung into full throttle.

The committee that had originally gathered to do this remake of *The Wizard of Oz* came up with a spectacular idea. They had decided to do their own thing by shooting in New York and urbanizing Oz. And so, as we shot what felt like my story in the very city I was living it, *The Wiz* became my therapy. New York City is so full of energy and things to do that it is an ideal place to stay busy and not feel sorry for yourself. I was not looking for a husband then, but I was looking for friends. Sidney Lumet, our director, became a very good friend to me and used to have wonderful dinner parties. He introduced me to a lot of his New York friends, and life became fuller and more interesting.

So I would shoot all day. When I could, I visited museums and libraries. I did whatever I had time for to immerse myself in the culture and bustle of New York. I went to movies, and then sometimes I would go dancing at Studio 54, a very trendy club owned by my friend Steve Rubell. This was a place where I could completely let myself go into the sound of music. When I wasn't dancing, there was a special place where I would sit up above the whole scene and watch what was going on. Studio 54 was a great place to be because the music was good and it was decorated in an exciting way. There were always celebrities going in and out, and although I wasn't there all that much, I did so love to go there occasionally to dance. I also went to dinner parties with other celebrities like Liza Minnelli, Halston, Iman and many other beautiful models, Andy Warhol, and various decorators and designers.

Although I now know it was going on, I was not aware of the drug scene at that time. I have been very lucky in my life to be able to steer myself away from drugs and the people who were involved with them. The music, the dancing, the aliveness, that was what attracted me. I loved that aspect of the nightlife, but I was not a party animal.

Most nights, after I put the kids to bed, I would read self-help materials, anything I could get my hands on to forget my pain and try to understand myself better. I stayed busy so that I wouldn't have time to think, but in truth, I was making life decisions: how to be alone and how to start over again. Although there was still a lot of internal pain, this time lives in my memory as a good one.

I had been greatly looking forward to the actual making of the film, for during the rehearsal time I felt that most of what we were doing was very special and unusual. I thought the idea was so great it couldn't miss. As I have found, there are many elements, both seen and unseen, that determine the success or failure of a film. Once we started shooting, I think that some of Sidney Lumet's artistic decisions resulted in a loss of the magical quality. It seemed to me that he could have used a spectacular and varied array of visual and technical special effects that were available to him, stunning things that would have created a much more magical effect for the viewers. Until the actual shooting began, I had been unaware of his concepts. I guess I had misjudged them and assumed that he and I shared a similar vision. Instead of moving into the full possibilities of what the world of film offers, he shot it as if it were a play. And he made it scary, more scary than I considered necessary or appropriate for children to watch. I always felt the fear factor was overdone; I never thought it needed to be so frightening. The faces of some of the characters were much too alarming. When my girls were small, I didn't let them watch it. It's the same with my boys today. I am very careful about what my children feed their minds, especially before they go to sleep. In the final analysis, there was a lot of fear in *The Wiz*. If you look closely, Dorothy was frightened every step of the way when she traveled the yellow brick road. I think it was too much fear to show children.

195

In my mind, the story itself redeemed the project. It was an important message. Although it was filled with fear and insecurity, it reached for a higher purpose as it resulted in transcending that fear and finding the inner worth. There I was, Dorothy, a shy Harlem kindergarten teacher, caught in a swirling blizzard, the chaos of my inner mind, and dropped into a scary wonderland. I have only my precious little dog Toto for a companion, and I must follow the yellow brick road to get home. Every step of the way is chock-full of metaphor, and the final message is positive and encouraging. It's about searching for something and then finding you've had it all along. Despite what it could have been, despite where I saw opportunities missed, the cast and crew were cooperative and helpful and I ended up considering it a completely worthwhile and enriching effort.

The annotated version of *The Wizard of Oz*, with its footnotes of literary and historical interest, talks about how the poppy fields were a representation of drugs. Sidney used those images when he placed us in the urban scene of the depraved part of New York City. We passed hookers hanging out on the streets, we walked through clouds of smoke, and by the time we left we were high, dizzy, and fogged over. I think he handled this aspect with tremendous subtlety and made it extremely interesting.

The costuming was done with a great deal of care. Such attention and intricate designing went into my simple little skirt and blouse! Every component was carefully thought out: which buttons to use, whether or not there would be ruffles, the color and style of Dorothy's hair and how it would complement the outfit. Each look for each character was taken very, very seriously.

I was given a relatively natural look, but the makeup for most of the other characters was extremely complex. The Lion makeup was created around Ted's own features, and he actually got to use a lot of his own face, but Michael's makeup was a different story. It was probably the most difficult of anyone's in the film, and it certainly took the most time to apply. I remember seeing poor little Michael, he was very young and inexperienced then, sitting there every morning for hours and hours, having his makeup painstakingly done and redone. And then there was the added difficulty of removing it every night, a process that must have been quite damaging to his skin, a possible source for the severe skin problems that he is presently experiencing and doesn't want to talk about.

One of the greatest joys of the filming was how close we all became, how much it felt like a family. We all fit together perfectly; it was a superb casting job. The lineup was impressive. Not only Michael, Ted, and Nipsey, but Lena Horne was the Good Witch. They were all a part of me.

Ted, the Cowardly Lion, was such a nice man to work with. I found him very much like the character he was playing, a gentle spirit who sometimes appeared as a big, mean old guy, but that was all illusion. He wasn't really like that. Nipsey, the Tinman, was a highly intelligent man, and he played someone who was extremely knowledgeable, used his logic brilliantly, but didn't feel, didn't have a heart, had never cried, and lacked sensitivity. It was a good part for Nipsey because although he was certainly not heartless, he had such a highly developed mind that he could easily relate to the role. And then there was Michael. The Scarecrow's thirst for knowledge, his desire to have a brain, to learn, to know more, was such a perfect mirror for Michael to reflect and express his life then. The four of us became very close during the shooting, and we also got to know each and every dancer and the choreographers. All in all, it was a lovely experience, but like life, it was not without its problems.

In one of the scenes, when we actually met the Wiz, I had to look straight into a huge light. I was supposed to be frightened, and so, as if I were almost paralyzed, I stared into the light with my eyes wide open for a long time. Of course we did takes and retakes as you always do in films, so I lost track of how many hours I gazed into the light. As usual, I threw myself completely into the scene and became mesmerized. It was not until I left the set that evening that I realized there was a blinding cover over my sore eyes and my sight was impaired. I was terribly upset and went straight to the doctor the next morning. After an extensive examination, he gave me some frightening news: I had burned the retinas of both eyes.

197

I had to stop working and was immediately checked into the hospital, where patches were placed over my eyes. There I lay, in a dark room for close to twenty-four hours, afraid I would never see again. The doctors told me when the retina is burned, there is no therapy to take care of it. It slowly heals by itself, and, depending upon the intensity of the burn, the process can take from a few days to many years to return to normal, if it ever does. I was lucky. Within a week, I was back to work and my eyesight was almost normal. I did sustain a dark spot in the center of one eye that is still there, but considering what the outcome could have been, I think I fared very well. During the week that I was out, my sister Rita filled in for me. Her skin is a little bit fairer than mine, but with the exception of her legs, her body looks a lot like mine from the back. So they cut her hair, and she did some of the shots for me. It was very sweet of her, and whenever I see those particular places in the film, I feel especially great love for her.

I also remember an animal tragedy on the set that was very sad for everyone. Several dogs had been hired to play the part of Toto, and these little puppies were kept in a room. One day, when they needed a dog for a particular scene, the propman entered the room and found a broken steampipe. One of the little Totos had been scalded very badly. All the puppies were rushed to the vet, but it was too late for the scalded puppy and he died. It was tragic for everyone. I had become very attached to my Totos.

We shot the entire film in and around New York and on soundstages at Astoria Studios. In fact, *The Wiz* was the first big production to open Astoria Studios. The film could not be considered a great financial success then or now, but success comes in many forms. When the filming was done, I was given my own soundstage at Astoria Studios, the Diana Ross soundstage, a wonderful studio in New York where movies continue to be made, where dreams can come true. A place after my own heart.

Even with the difficulties and the places where, in my estimation, the film came up short, the end result was a good one. I made friends, I learned and I grew, I made positive life changes. My life was expanding, becoming happier and more meaningful. I was taking my power, both as a woman and as a performer. The long-suffered emptiness within me was filling up, and by the time the film was done, I, like Dorothy, had found that everything I was searching for was right there with me all along. I just had to believe in myself and set myself free. And finally, I was doing it.

> *Can't you feel a brand-new day?*
> *Everybody be glad,*
> *Because the sun is shining just for us.*
> *Everybody wake up.*
> *Hello, World.*
> *It's like a different way of living now.*

It's My Turn

The first level under — what you see
onstage
under the stage
backstage
behind the curtains
under the rug
in my heart
losing myself
finding myself

Leaving Motown was a profound experience. The truth is that I did not leave Motown because I was upset or angry or hurt. I left because I was growing as a person and it was time for me to move on.

In the spring of 1980, Nile Rodgers and Bernard Edwards, a very talented songwriting team, sat down with me to talk about my career and what was happening in my life. "I'm Coming Out" was the result of that meeting. It was released in August of 1980, and it was a true reflection of my feelings then. I can't say that I had a premonition that I was getting ready to leave Motown, in fact I did not, but I knew that I was getting ready to change in a big way. You know the feeling, when you're unhappy and although you don't know what's about to happen, you know that things can't go on the way they are. That was how it felt for me then.

OPPOSITE PAGE:
I've taken pictures with some of the world's greatest photographers.
This is a Victor Skrebneski portrait of me as Josephine Baker.

This kind of spiritual insight is something I have always had, an instinctual knowing when something is in the air, when something new is about to occur. I have it right now, as I write this book. I guess it is one of the reasons I am writing my memoirs at this time. I feel a shift about to happen, and I can only hope it will be all positive and wonderful.

Perhaps my music is part of what has clued me in to when these changes are brewing. At some point in my career, it began to feel as if the music and I were one, either the songs were following me around or I was following the songs. In 1980, just prior to my leaving Motown, I had three big hits, two of which were directly expressing my life: "I'm Coming Out" was the first one. Then, one month later, "It's My Turn," a beautiful song written by a great songwriter named Michael Masser, was released. Michael, who also wrote "Touch Me in the Morning" and "Do You Know Where You're Going To?," the theme from *Mahogany*, was a very difficult man to work with, maybe because he knew how fabulous he was, but he surely could write songs that were relevant. "It's My Turn" became very important to me. Apparently, I wasn't the only one who felt that way. After it was released, I heard from a lot of other women who told me they strongly connected and identified with that particular song. They must have been in the same position I was in because they would say to me, "Were you really going through the same things I was going through at the time?"

"Probably so," I would answer. It was a collective experience. And the lyrics were stated so succinctly:

I can't cover up my feelings in the name of love.

Just that. Plain and simple. Besides the fact that the feelings were so clearly defined, what I love best about this song is the strength that it expresses.

It's my turn, I don't have all the answers,
But at least I know I'll take my share of chances.

I often wonder what would have happened to me if I hadn't gone out on my own, if I hadn't made the decision to step up and take my share of chances. It did not look as if this would be an easy transition, but I had to do something. I had reached a point where I wasn't learning anything because someone was always doing everything for me. My friend Suzanne de Passe was growing more powerful every day and becoming a better and better producer. She was experimenting and learning her craft, but I was not.

"Okay, go on out there, sing your songs, wear your gowns, look pretty, we'll do the rest." That was basically the message Motown was always giving me. As I followed their directives, I was stagnating. I got caught up in the mode of allowing everybody else to take care of my life. After all, they made everything so easy. They did my finances, they paid my taxes, they bought my house, and I never had to figure out any of these things for myself. It was a seductive lifestyle. Somewhere in there, I decided that enough was enough. I felt that I had to start doing for myself.

When you make a film, you have a director. He tells you what to do, and you act accordingly because he is supposed to see the bigger picture. That was why he was hired for the job. Well, that might work in a film, but life is not a movie. We human beings have minds of our own; we are not puppets to be pushed and pulled at somebody else's whim. I have my own thoughts about things, I have my own opinions, and what I finally decide is right for me may not coincide with what you have in mind. That's just the way free will works, but I had given up my free will.

All of these people were making decisions for me, and I had no voice. I felt completely disempowered; everybody was telling me what to do. Suddenly, I couldn't take it anymore. It was as if one day my eyes opened up and I thought to myself, "I can do some of that stuff, I can choose my own songs and even help write them. I could produce my own television shows." What a concept! Before this realization, I had stayed in the same passive mode for a long time and refused to do it any differently. Even before my divorce, I was learning and getting wiser. Many things were different after the move to California; I was really starting to change.

And so was Berry, but not necessarily for the better. He had the same sharp mind he always had, but he had begun to act like a genius gone mad. He had always been a dominating person, but his control issues were escalating. He was reaching the place where he was always right and everybody around him was always wrong. He had gone from being a person I admired and happily consulted with to someone who wouldn't listen. I could never get in a word edgewise. I guess the adage "Power corrupts" is true. It was certainly true in Berry Gordy's case. Somewhere along the line, he must have forgotten that he was a leader, not a dictator. He made it unbearable for me, and so, inadvertently, he became for me an instrument of change.

I am so grateful that I was able to break free. I guess once you've cared for someone, it's hard to change. In many ways, I feel sorry that it went bad. If it were possible, he would probably still be controlling me from his grave in some ways.

Each of us must fight our own battles. It wasn't easy for me to break free. Ultimately, I had to free myself. I had difficulty in discerning whether or not I even wanted my freedom. I remember how protectively I used to react when anybody said anything against Berry. Shades of it are still with me today. I know that he gave me my start.

Berry had a powerful business instinct. I can't really imagine where it came from, how he became such an expert. He built Motown from scratch, and whatever he was earning he put right back into the business. In this way, Berry was putting our money back into us. He paid for our training, the finishing schools, the Artistic Development programs he set up to train us. Motown was a family experience, and it gave us things that our real families couldn't. Everyone was able to travel and see the world. The money for all of that had to come from somewhere, especially in the beginning, when a hit song paid almost nothing compared to how it all works today. It would be so easy to tear Berry down by saying, "He always tried to tell me what to do, he was such a tyrant, he worked us too hard." But then I wonder, if he hadn't pushed us, if he hadn't made us work, would we have stuck with it? Would any other record company have taken the time with us to develop our talents like he did? I don't think so, I really don't. And so I never felt ripped off. For me, I think that it all balanced out in the end. I'm not speaking for anyone else.

When I left Motown, in my heart I said, "Okay. We're even." And I really meant it. I felt that he had built his company and sold it for millions of dollars. Money isn't everything. I had built my name, and, reciprocally, we had helped each other do these things. At the time, I just wanted to go on from there and make the best of it all. I don't get off on moaning and complaining about what I should have had or what I could have had. I don't believe in that kind of behavior. For me, complaining does nothing to support future movement. I don't believe in blaming other people for my own experiences. I left happy to have been part of a wonderful dream. How Berry felt was probably a different story. I know that he really didn't want to let go.

When I was finally on my own, I was pretty vulnerable in the outside world. I had a barrelful of problems, and it took me a long time to get them all sorted out. The simple pleasures that were now mine soon overwhelmed the troubles. Like planning my own life. It was definitely a challenge to stay out of the fear and negativity. When *The Wiz* was finished, I was having trouble finding a new film project for myself and I remember thinking, "I have a choice here. I can walk around saying, 'There are no film projects for blacks or women.' Or I can use my head and figure out how to invest in myself and create my own projects." I chose the latter. Rather than complaining about what I couldn't do, I decided to start my own production company. Being able to do what I wanted in my own time was worth every inch of the hard road I traveled to get there.

I worked hard to make myself a beautiful career. Success is not all that it is cracked up to be. It can be lonely and isolating, but I learned that it was up to me to make of it what I wanted. I can complain about being alone or I can deal with it and use the alone time to think and study and learn. Once again, the quality of my life in each moment is completely up to me.

When I took the big leap, when I left Motown and went out on my own, all I really wanted is the same thing I want now: to be in charge of myself and my life. I don't need to be in charge of anybody else, I've

205

seen how that turns out, but I want to be responsible for my own destiny. Then, if things work out, I can feel accomplished, and if they don't, I can at least know I tried. And then I can try again.

I had always been intrigued by Josephine Baker. She was indeed one of a kind—a woman of vision, determination, and courage who looked at the world as it was and found a way to make it better. At least that's the way I have always seen her. She was such an enigma to the world. There are so many different stories about her, no one knows for sure who she really was. She lived in a society that practiced hate and bigotry, so she created her own world, adopting children of every race and practically every nationality to live together in a town that she more or less owned in the southwest of France, not far from Bordeaux.

Back in the late seventies and early eighties, I decided I wanted to make the story of Josephine Baker's life, the first major project of the film division of my corporation, and I started negotiations for distribution with Paramount Pictures. I was to star as Josephine, truly one of the most fascinating women ever in show business. It was a perfect vehicle for me.

To begin with, she was an extraordinary entertainer who added exotic touches to her performances. She pumped her personality into her act, sometimes clowning, sometimes appearing nearly nude in elaborately made costumes with headpieces that seemed to live a fantasy of their own. Every major designer in Paris longed to clothe La Baker, among them, Christian Dior and Jacques Griffe.

She was an incredible woman who did so much more than we Americans knew about. The work she performed for racial equality was worldwide. Though her dream was to become successful in America, she could never become a major star here. Yet in Europe she really was regarded as a very special human being. They loved her in Europe and took care of her. She became close friends with many European dignitaries, including royalty, nobility, presidents, and dictators. When she died, she was given a state funeral.

I pushed very hard for this project because it was a dream for me and I really, deeply believe that dreams do come true. Often, they might not come when you want them. They come in their own time.

Childbirth and having babies
have been the most magical
times for me.

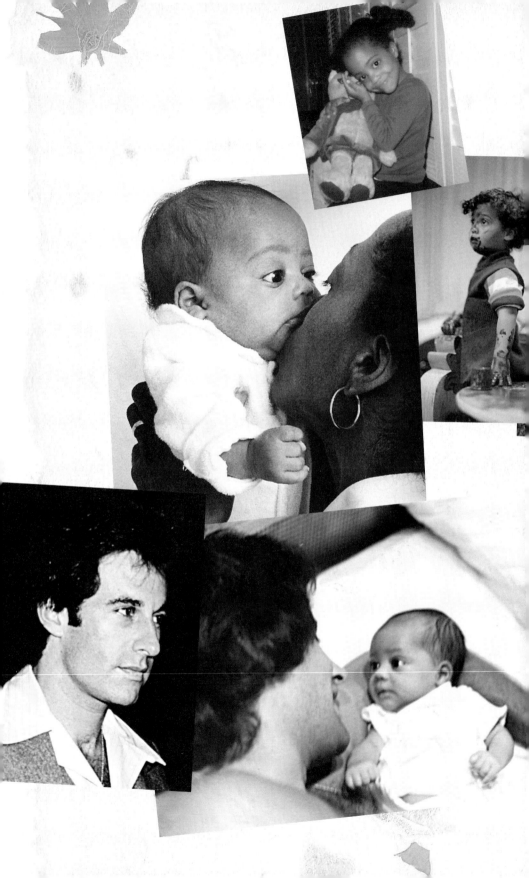

The essence of who I am is more a mother, wife, and friend than a celebrity.

A breath, a cry
New sounds
Strangers all around
And two of them belong to me
I think one is Mommy,
I chose them, the other is Bob
He likes to be called Daddy, but,
I'm not going to talk yet.
They wanted a boy, but they'll take what they get.
Rhonda and Tracee and me, Chudney Lane Silberstein
When we grow up Mommy says we can be The Supremes
Oh, I almost forgot—I weighed 7-13.
Born Nov. 4, 1975

Written by Suzanne de Passe

My greatest gifts in life have been my children.

Life is wonderful, yet there are still so many things I want to do and see.

I'm proud of what I've achieved. It reminds me of how blessed I am and that I want to give more of myself to others.

The Josephine Baker project has been a series of setbacks. I spent a decade trying to get someone to do a movie with me as star. By 1980 or 1981, I decided just to go ahead and do it myself because nothing was happening. The movie business was undergoing changes in terms of what filmgoers wanted to see and what Hollywood wanted to put out. This was a time of *Star Wars*, *Raiders of the Lost Ark*, and *E.T.* Of course, there also were a few noteworthy epics made at that time such as *Gandhi* and *Reds* and a few lighter treats like *Victor/Victoria* and *Tootsie*. This was when I got married and started having babies again, so my energies were divided.

I continued to try, but I kept having difficulty selling my dream to the big studios. I was going to a thousand meetings. Since I couldn't get things off the ground here, I went to Paris, found myself an apartment, and started seeing different people who might finance the movie there.

I spent a lot of time researching Josephine's life. She had a sort of raw, natural energy and high sense of style and elegance that made her stand out from all the other performers in the Folies-Bergère, where she starred. Her color made her an even greater star because the Europeans, unlike the Americans, loved the fact that she was a Negro. When World War II came, Josephine sang to raise money for war relief and worked with the Free French forces. When she finally returned to the United States to perform, she would do so only if blacks and whites could sit together in the same audience. Although she lived abroad, she quietly fought racial discrimination on every level, even forcing a stagehands' union to integrate by threatening not to perform. She retired in 1956 but went back to work so she could raise funds for the orphanage she built in France for children from all over the world. She herself adopted twelve children.

Not having made the Josephine Baker movie is quite sad for me because it is like a lost dream. I am not sure what will happen with the project, but whatever comes about, I know I have given it my best shot. My ambitions have not ended with one project or seemingly the death of one dream. They are very much alive.

Many people view ambition as a negative quality in an individual. I do not think ambition is bad; it's just my life force, who I am. I cannot stop—Josephine Baker could not stop. She kept going until the day she died, which was during the second night of a triumphal return to the stage.

Time is moving too fast, and I have too many things I want to do. I think once you stop wanting to create, wanting to work and push forward, you become old. And then you die.

As long as you have goals and ambition, your spirit is alive and your energy still flows. As you continue to watch the possible opportunities open up for you as you travel your journey of life, you either take advantage of them or you do not. You make choices all the time. If you are lucky enough, you make the right choices.

Did Josephine make the right choices? That was for her to know, but I believe she did. Did I make the right choices? Yes, I know I did.

The Magical
Light of Dusk

The eighties were about creating a brand-new life. I spent most of it alone, being a single parent to my girls. It was a time of searching: for more of myself, for more understanding of what I wanted and what would make me happy, and for a permanent home for my kids.

I was truly not looking for a man. I did enjoy some companionship with men, I dated off and on, but a husband was out of the question then. I was too busy soothing past pains, healing old wounds, and finding a new direction for my career. This entire cycle of renewal lasted nine years, starting with my divorce from Bob until I met Arne Naess in 1984. Although I had already begun the task of taking responsibility for my life, it deepened greatly during this period. I had been singing for more than twenty years, and although I knew a great deal about the ins and outs of performing, there were so many areas of life in which I was a novice. I decided to change that. And so I used this time to educate myself by learning more about the things that I had neglected over the past two decades, particularly business and finances.

Over the years, I have been heavily involved in the business world, and I think I have become pretty good at it. I've involved myself in many business interests, some of which did not work out very well and some of which did. I think that real estate has been my best investment to date. I bought an office building in New York, five floors of which I used to create my companies: Anaid Films, Ross Records, Ross Town, Ross Publishing Company, and my own financial department called RTC Management Corporation. I kept the building for two and a half

OPPOSITE PAGE:
The eighties were about creating a brand-new life.
They were a time of looking within.

years and then sold it for a good profit. I moved my offices into a smaller space after learning that I needed fewer people to make my organization work than when I began. I also learned that having good legal assistance is crucial, so I employed the best legal advice I could find. I had many mentors over the years in different areas of business: real estate, investments, stocks.

In 1980, I went full swing into business for myself. I had the vision and the dream of what I wanted to do, so I built a staff of very creative people, very much as it was in the beginning of Motown. I hired the best people I could find, people who knew more than I did, people from whom I could learn to create businesses that would work. In these areas, it was the street education that was most important, especially in music. I found highly creative people who knew everything about the music and film industries, videos, and computers to help me.

My music has grown right along with the industry. The technologies in the fields of film and music are moving very rapidly, and we must always keep one step ahead of ourselves. I have had to understand the speed of this business, to visualize what's going to happen next and push myself out into the future. Vinyl LPs and 45s and even cassettes are just about gone. Now we're on to CDs, DAT machines, and digital equipment. The idea is to learn quickly and expand your vision to the unexpected, almost as if it's science fiction. That's how fast the industry is moving. That's why I wrote "Back to the Future."

Since the early sixties, my voice has traveled to smaller and larger places than I could ever have imagined. The world has been our market. Japan, the Far East, Africa, Europe, the United Kingdom, and Germany are all big markets for music. The trick is to be able to distribute to all the different areas of the world.

My first record deal after I left Motown was with RCA. Although there were many exciting things about that deal, the best part was working with Bob Summers and John Frankenheimer, my lawyer. I was given the complete opportunity to produce my own records, from finding the musicians to setting up studio time, mixing, mastering, layering the music onto the tracks, finding the engineer, overseeing the photographs, creating the title, doing the colors for the cover, choosing the costumes, the names, the liner notes, every single ingredient. I also inspected the label copying, the layouts for the jacket, selected the release dates, and most important, sat through hours and hours of producing. It was a magnificent learning experience. I loved it then and I still do, but today I must use my time differently. I have found that sitting through the editing is not the best place for me. It sometimes makes it difficult to be objective, so I allow the engineers to do the mixing, while I retain the creative objective point of view.

When I worked with RCA, I selected the musicians and I knew them. I talked about the music as it evolved, told them how I felt about the music, how the particular musician was playing it, whether it was the percussionist, the guitar player, or the synthesist. This was extremely important. I was able to make sure that there was a freedom in the music within a certain amount of restriction and that there was air, that there was space. To me, it is the space between the notes that makes music. When the music is too cluttered and full, it becomes difficult to hear and understand. Then it is messy, with no beginning and no end. By the time I got to actually record, something had already been put together for me and I just laid on my vocal.

213

I have found that it is all about trusting your instincts. If you keep getting good at something, and if you organize very well, then people will recognize your expertise and you will be supported in moving on. For instance, my film producing is an extension of my being organized and being professional.

I am an idea person in every area: films, stories, how things should look. It's another of my God-given gifts. It's certainly nothing that I ever studied. You can develop your talents and help them grow, but studying cannot produce innate talents. When I simply trust my hunches, I go out beyond my limits.

Around this time, Lionel Richie wanted to launch his solo career. He had had tremendous success as part of his group, Lionel Richie and the Commodores, much the same as I had had with the Supremes. He was an incredible songwriter, and now he was looking to do a duet in order to introduce himself as a solo artist. I was already a solo performer, and when we recorded his song "Endless Love" together, I was the vehicle in supporting his launch. He wrote the song for the movie, and although *Endless Love* did not do well, the song was brilliant and, as with *Mahogany*, the song did better than the film.

The working relationship between us was difficult. I am a perfectionist. I like to be on time *always*. Lionel was not always on time. I did work very well, however, with the producer, James Carmichael, who is also a perfectionist. He knows music and voice tonality, and he can hear sound quality like nobody else. He is a great talent, and "Endless Love" became a huge hit.

I have learned to surround myself with the right kinds of people, I'm not afraid to ask a lot of questions, and I place great attention on details. It's important to hold off making final decisions until you have done the research, until you have all the background information. Once the decision is made, if you find that you have made a mistake, then it is important not to dwell on the past but to move right on to the next opportunity. My life has been rich with opportunities and I have tried to keep looking forward.

One of my greatest tools has been my positive-thinking tapes. I use them constantly, they are a great source of inspiration, and I'm not embarrassed to let people know how much they inspire me and assist me in maintaining my self-esteem. It is important to feel motivated and enthusiastic, to keep a good self-image and dream the impossible.

Although I have focused my attention on being a good businesswoman, I have always had a natural business sense. It's just something that came with the package. My parents were organized; they could figure things out and deal with problems. Along with what I learned from them, much of my business expertise came from reading books, which I turn to for new information. I didn't go to business classes, and I didn't learn about economics in school. I learned initially from my own childhood that you can be raised in a poor neighborhood and still have an opportunity to use your mind and grow.

My business ability is clear. I have become a good negotiator because I am not afraid to talk about money. Over the years I have made a lot of mistakes, but I'd rather not blame anybody. I'd rather be personally responsible for not having had the knowledge. Then I can make the appropriate changes. I know many celebrities and show-business people who hand their financial matters over to someone else. I would rather learn and do it myself. Knowledge is power. I keep on learning how to make my money work for me. I think I am fairly frugal with money. I certainly believe in having a good life, I love beautiful things, but I buy things that I think will last. I love to travel and to work hard.

I also love education. As an adult, I have attended night classes at the New School in New York. I took a film finance class. Somebody got up on the first night and said, "Well, I know why I'm here, but I want to know why Diana Ross is here." I was there because it was no longer good enough to let someone else handle my finances. Film finance is very difficult to understand, and I needed an understanding of it for myself. I wanted to know how to use a computer, how to make deals. I won't put my name on a contract unless I understand exactly what I am signing. I sign all my own checks. I find that to be an area of great importance.

Finally, I am keenly aware of image. I want very much to be a good role model for women, for all young people, and particularly for my race. Too much wonderful young talent and intellect is being lost today. I want to be instrumental in inspiring young people to come forward, to trust themselves, and to utilize their intelligence and education to improve their lives.

When I initially moved to New York, it was a time of letting go of many loose ties. Sadly, this included friends and people I loved, especially the people who had supported me in my career and helped me build my wonderful life. But I had to let go. It was time for me to move on from them, and I found that tremendously painful.

Being a single parent was not hard for me. It became an incredible release because I didn't have to answer to anyone. This was a new and much desired state of being for me at the time. I was on my own raising my girls, so I was free to make my own choices and to do what came to me naturally. My mother proved to be a fantastic support during those years. She would come to help me with the girls when I had to leave for career obligations and also when I went on tour. Since the apartment was small, I needed only a housekeeper to help me run things and assist me with child care and a driver to get my children to school every morning. The kids didn't want a chauffeur to drive them to school because it made them feel uncomfortable. They wanted to take the bus. Many mornings, I would actually ride on the bus with them to make sure they traveled safely and got off at the right stop. It was fun riding the bus, it was so normal. I loved being with my girls and the other children, too, and so my memories of those times are happy ones.

I've always been a bit of a loner, and I enjoy spending time by myself and with my children. I maintained some of the friendships I made at that time. Millie Kaiserman, whom I met while I was living in New York, is a dear and supportive woman who has remained a close friend. She was very good to me and to my children. Apart from a few special people, I was alone a lot. You stop being invited to parties if you never attend them. I began to record and produce my own songs. Even when I'm not traveling, there's never any real downtime.

Although living in New York can be romantic and exciting for a single woman, I felt it was a frightening place to raise kids. Right from the start, I knew that the apartment and the city were temporary. After about a year, I began to look for a real home in a lovely place that was close to nature with living trees and grass instead of apartment buildings, concrete, and taxis. I did not want to have to travel two to three hours to get back and forth, so it would have to be somewhere close, just on the outskirts of the city. That way, I would have easy access to the city when I needed it, and yet I would still have a healthy place to raise my children. I wanted the best of both worlds.

> *When I think of home, I think about a place*
> *Where there's love overflowing.*

That line from *The Wiz* will always stay with me. It was my guiding light during my search for a wonderful home. And I found it.

When I first saw my future home, it was the grounds and trees that spoke to me. In fact, as beautiful as the house is, I never even went inside until I had walked the grounds. I was entranced; I felt an instant communion with nature there. I love being close to nature, a passion that turns out to be one of the strongest connections between my husband, Arne, and me. His first love and his life's work are ecology, and I remember showing the land to him when we met. He appreciated the beauty, it would be difficult not to, but he said to me, "This is not real nature because it's not natural. It's planted and manicured. Real nature is the forest and the lakes and the mountains." In the purest sense, he was right, but this land was and still remains a nature connection for me.

We talked about our childhoods and how were brought up, I explained to him the difficulties of growing up in Detroit, where it was all concrete and alleyways. I don't recall having seen many trees there, and grass was practically nonexistent. Even when I lived in California, I had no real grounds at my home, only a front lawn. Here, in my new home, it was different. I knew almost immediately that I wanted the house and I purchased it, even though I had no idea how I would afford it. It was a big risk, but it just felt right.

The acreage around my house was once rich in bluestone. Stone was 217 blasted from the face of the cliffs, then cut and sledded nearby to the quarry's dock on Byram Cove. Once there, it was loaded for shipment on large sailing schooners. Not all of it was exported. It is said that the stone for the Brooklyn Bridge footings and the beautiful pedestal that supports the Statue of Liberty herself were mined from this area, possibly this very farm. There is no doubt that countless New York buildings claim their strength from bluestone, the very stone that was blasted from these cliffs.

The farm was not only prospering as a stone quarry. During World War II, many adjustments were made to life on the farm. The main house was closed to conserve heating fuel, and the family moved its residence into the old Quarry cottage. The farming operations, previously minimal, took on new importance in the war effort, and Quarry Farm was unsurpassed in food production.

Most of the money to maintain the land was made in bluestone, and as always, progress changed things. As concrete became so much cheaper and more available for building material, bluestone became obsolete and the land lost its viability as a quarry. In 1918, the artist and architect Paul Chalfin bought the nine acres of land for his personal enjoyment. It is said that several movies were shot on the grounds. The quarry's cliffs are the exquisite backdrop for Pearl White's *The Perils of Pauline* and several other films. The site was then used for dramatic and musical productions. This intrigued me. The estate held a wonderful history. I feel a great magic, living on my small farm. My kids just love it.

In the 1950s, the construction of the Connecticut Turnpike caused the farm to be divided. My research of the time says it was turned into what was called a "play farm," for farming vegetables. There were also apple, peach, and cherry trees, and much of the acreage was used as pastureland for cows and horses and a small dairy farm. The bottles of milk carried the farm's name.

Ventilation was added to the outdoor cottage, which was modeled on the smokehouse at George Washington's home at Mount Vernon, and sweet woods were used to smoke meat. Exquisite gardens were designed and managed with care as meticulous as that done for the farm.

The house was designed as a French Normandy–style chateau. It was originally enclosed by a six-foot-high stone wall. Over the years, different hands remodeled the house, giving it a steep slate roof and tall brick chimneys. The dramatic touch of a spiral staircase swirling from the basement to the third floor was added. Fine, antique woodwork, much of which was imported from Europe, can be found all through the house. The living room has eighteenth-century wood paneling, and there are parquet floors in several of the rooms. There is actually an organ room on the ground floor, a cold-storage room, and the pièce de résistance—a one-lane bowling alley in the basement.

Picture the magical light of dusk settling upon the inlet that you can see from the grounds of my beautiful home. I walk across the lush lawns and smell the fragrant flowers. I walk past the Japanese maple trees that are dripping with oversized pink blossoms and head toward the edge of the water. This was a long way from 5736 St. Antoine and a long way from the confusion I had been through. I am so thankful to be able to be a part of this beautiful land. God has really been good to me.

Interiors

Still Places

Success can be lonely — isolating
disappointing
you don't get used to it.
you deal with it and use it
make it helpful — thinking time
I call it.

When I am lonely, using my imagination gets me through. When I was a teenager, I used to pretend I was in a different country, a different world, anywhere except where I was. I'd look at pictures and just push myself in—I'd go to wonderful places and explore. That's why it's never been hard being alone. I just go someplace else. I'm really a dreamer, and being able to dream and travel have kept me happy. There are still places I want to go. If you ever get lonely, travel. If you can't afford the trip, rip out pictures in magazines and pretend. No one needs to know.

I understand loneliness is a part of the human condition, and everyone is a little lonely every now and then. We shouldn't spend all our time and energy focused on how alone we might be at the time because this only drains our spirit. Keeping busy helps—filling up your life with things to do. The world is filled with so many wonders. There is so much to do no matter where you live: in a city, on a farm, in the suburbs,

OPPOSITE PAGE:
Now that I am older, I have learned to appreciate my solitude.

OVERLEAF:
The world is there for you to see and experience. Travel as much as you can.
Meet different people and learn about their lives, cultures, and feelings, because
education comes not only from books and classrooms.

a forest, a beach, a desert. Anyplace offers some form of challenge and an infinite variety of things to do.

I have a lot of interests, and when I get lonely, I just get busy. Sometimes I read a book. Reading, like imagination, can take you anywhere. Books can open new doors; they can be companions and bring new adventures. So no one ever needs to be lonely. Instead, we can embrace life and seek out new activities, new challenges. We can learn to enjoy the specialness of ourselves. You can be your own best friend, your most enjoyable companion.

I guess loneliness comes and goes in a person's life. It helps to be aware of those moments in your life when you might be particularly vulnerable or open to feeling low. When I feel really in despair and when I feel lonely, I first try to consider my health: Maybe I need more vitamins; maybe I haven't had enough sleep. Perhaps I had too much to eat or drink or have an allergy or am catching a cold. I always think that something physically different is causing me to think so blue, so I check my health first and work on my physical being. I try to find the best ways to change the feelings. First, I look for those things that will give me a lift. I might have to force myself to take action, but if I give myself positive encouragement, I see positive results.

I seek ways within myself to gain self-control, to be in charge of my destiny and learn how to look for the signs, how to cope with all the external nuisances that can disturb my inner core. For many people, loneliness usually strikes when they should be doing something other than what they are doing, or when they are idle, or when they feel left out and are just not doing things that make them happy or fulfilled. My loneliness comes when I'm bored or frustrated.

Working is an important part of my life. I started working at a young age, and I've always been doing something. Now that I am older, I have learned to appreciate my solitude. I cherish those moments when I can be by myself because so much of my life has been spent surrounded by so many people. Now, I often like the comfort of being alone, of eating alone, of sleeping alone. Many people think of being alone as a sad thing, but there are two sides to that coin. I have learned the difference between loneliness and being by myself. Loneliness is more emotional and sometimes can set off physical distress. It is an all-consuming emptiness, almost like being turned inside out and watching your spirit blow away.

There is a certain loneliness attached to single parenthood. I got used to it for the nine years I was a single mother to my girls. I got used to being the decision maker because I had to be. That was the reality. I couldn't sit back and say, "Somebody, help me make this decision." Single parenthood encourages strength because you carry all the responsibility and try to be everything for your children. There's no one else to pick up the slack.

> I was shivering
> my legs were shaking
> I didn't think they could hold me
> I had to sit down
> people were talking but
> I couldn't hear — it felt as if they
> were in a dream.
>
> I was inside my head
> I wasn't there really
> I felt I was this little voice
> inside of my body
> deep inside
> maybe this is what people
> feel when they are in a coma
>
> Here I am — here inside
> can't you hear me
> I know you see me
> I'm right here —
> but my mouth wasn't moving
> my legs wouldn't move
> I couldn't get out — I couldn't get up
> was I lying down or floating

223

I wanted to run but I couldn't
I heard my scream and I woke up

I was dreaming – oh my
It was a scary dream
but I've had it before
anxiety. what am I afraid of
I'm shaking and I am cold
am I scared and what of –
dying. I demand to live
a long time – I wanna be here
I try to breathe slowly
I get up – walk around the house
looking for I don't know what –
is everyone here
safe and sleeping
I look around my room

I'm on my side of the bed
his side – untouched waiting
for him to be there

Loneliness is an explosion of fear—if you let it get you. As much as I love being around my children and husband, I sometimes look forward to being alone, especially when I'm on the road. When I'm by myself in hotel rooms, I can be myself and be real. I don't have to try to dress up during the day if I don't want to. I don't have to wear makeup, or look alert, or comb my hair, or act a special way for somebody. These things become life's little luxuries—the glory of just doing nothing, of indulging myself with small pleasures.

Despite my quiet enjoyment of solitude, I miss my children and husband. Yearnings run deep inside me. I want to be with them. I need to be with them. With the children, I even begin to feel guilty. I start to think that the person watching them is not taking care of them the way I would and is not paying attention to all the things that I would if I were there. I talk to my children all the time when I am on the road. And I form pictures in my head of how their faces look while we talk. I envision their expressions, and I can almost see their little hands holding the phone. Ever since Ross and Evan were born, almost six years ago, I have tried to stay home and off the road as much as possible so I can be with them every day.

Being alone has allowed me to grow more inside, to evolve spiritually and emotionally. I know that whatever is making me feel bad is not going to last forever unless I allow it to. Tomorrow it will be better. I do whatever it takes to change my life around. I don't collapse into despair or wallow in the blues. There are highs, and there are lows. One thing I know is that the dark periods of my life have humbled me and have given me positive lessons. Goodness can come from adversity. I try to stay still inside, deeply feel my feelings, and keep loving myself.

Light over Darkness

I hope you're hearing my prayers in Heaven
I dream with a child's faith
we all need help
I sometimes feel discouraged
needing wings to fly away
'cause nobody knows me
nobody really sees me

Life is wonderful
there are things I want to see and remember
my moments are sacred

The possibilities of saving lives
fighting the rich and mean
I'm riding the sound of a train
to happiness

Relationships, like people, undergo changes and require care and attention. Nurturing those relationships helps our friendships grow. I have found that if we treat others as we would like to be treated, the goodness we give to our friends will be returned. I have always had a few very dear, close friends, but I have also been alone a lot. I have wanted it that way. I have needed the time to delve deeply into my spirituality and my personal growth work. Whenever that aloneness

OPPOSITE PAGE:
I try not to dwell on the past, but your past is a part of who you are.

shifts into loneliness, it never lasts long because I keep the love of my friends in my heart.

In my childhood, things were different than they are now. I remember Sharon Burstyn, my girlfriend who was Smokey Robinson's niece. We spent lots of time together, but we weren't very close. I had no one at that time to whom I could hold on or with whom I could identify. Today, that has changed. I have close friendships that are extremely important to me. My friends are people who are just there, not asking for any returns. In my life, real friendships, whether they are with men or women, are like platonic love affairs. I have noticed that my girls have male friends with whom they get together and really talk. I like this kind of sharing, but in my life it has been rare.

Dealing with Mary Wilson's book was a journey in which lightness triumphed over darkness. I was depressed for a while, but as I have said, I don't hold on to bad feelings. I loved Mary. She and I started out as good friends. That's what I remember most. My love for her didn't end one day because she wrote a book. I can't love you on Monday, then Tuesday you're not so good, so I don't love you anymore. I have told my children that everyone loves them when they're good. That's easy. But I will always love them, even when they're bad. That's real love.

I have forgiven Mary. She was my dear friend and I never stopped loving her, but I had to let go of her. It hurt too much. Forgiving someone doesn't necessarily mean I have to be with that person. I wish Mary only good things in life, but I no longer consider her a friend. It seems that I have cared too much in my relationships. I had to allow our friendship to fade away.

It was very hard for me to make a final emotional break from Mary, but it had to be done. I never stand still because if you're not moving forward, you're probably moving backward. I don't ever regret loving, even if it didn't turn out well. I guess it's better to trust and be disappointed once in a while than to distrust and be miserable all the time. Still, some events in my life have been hard to accept.

What makes someone feel like a true friend? I think it is the ease in communication, the feeling of not being afraid to trust someone with your heart and your most private feelings. Suzanne de Passe is a true longtime friend. We share many thoughts and feelings. We've drifted apart lately because of our careers and logistics, but I know she cares about me. And she knows I care about her. We used to talk about everything, especially Berry Gordy. More recently, we've shared some really good times together, like our weddings and my babies.

I'd love to have more girlfriends at this time in my life, but I guess I don't trust very easily. My separateness, my aloneness, has always been here and is here now, a recurring theme that has continuously run through my life. My closeness with Mama didn't change it. My five siblings didn't change it. Growing up in our small apartment in the projects didn't change it, either. Aloneness is an inner state; it can show up in a huge crowd. Even now, with my three beautiful daughters, my two sweet young sons, and my wonderful, sexy husband, deep down inside, I am still profoundly alone.

Standing Tall
Through It All

Maybe I had finally made it to the top. The top—there's nothing at the top except the top. I've never really wanted to feel that I had made it because, then, what is there to work toward?

Working is an important part of my life. I simply do not know any other way to live. Deadlines and goals are important to me. In fact, when I think about retiring, I grow cold because I never want to. I really wouldn't know what to do with myself. I don't know why I am this way. I feel there is so little time in life.

My life has always been my family and music.

In my career, music is my foundation. Although I have had many other business interests and pursued other activities and projects, it always has been my love of music that's been the source of my energy.

Singing—performing—is a gift. A divine gift. To be able to touch people all over the world with a record or a concert is truly a miracle. I hope I have been able to use this gift well by using my music to help people feel good, to help people feel alive, proud, and happy about their lives.

Those are some of the things music has done for my life. Music lifts my spirits and gives me joy. And always, music makes me want to move. I love to dance. I love music that makes me feel good, so it is natural that I am drawn to dance music. My tastes in music stay contemporary because I listen to what my children play. I love listening to the radio and hearing what's new and good. Music I admire automatically influences music I record and perform.

OPPOSITE PAGE:
Singing . . . performing . . . is a gift. A divine gift.

Onstage, I like to move with the songs, to be a canvas upon which the lighting can paint. The band is there with me while I'm moving to the music. I have been lucky enough to have the greatest musicians in the business, and I always want to be able to show them off.

Being in front of an audience is like floating through heaven with a smile on your face. An audience gives you such incredible energy. It can embrace you, make you feel warm, and make you forget all the pain and sorrow you might have at the time. Although physical pain is always easy to handle onstage, I have found it very hard to let go of emotional pain while I perform.

As you know by now, dwelling on the positive has been the motivating force in my being able to grow and learn as an entertainer and as a human being. A positive attitude, dedication, and determination have been the tapestry of my life. But it seems that with every achievement, with every move I have made, no matter how great or small, someone was always there to try to bring me down. I have been criticized every step of the way. I have been called names; my music has been ridiculed and my movies taken apart.

This has been true as far back as I can recall. When I was a child, I remember how I had practiced and practiced to be in a school play. I wanted so badly to sing in this little production. A teacher I had, Mr. Scrimsher, discouraged me. He was very condescending. Although he never said it, I got the feeling he wanted to tell me, "Don't try to do this. Do something else—go get a menial job or something." I think that put-down made me want to prove him wrong.

I have always looked at the positive qualities of criticism. Constructive criticism helped me grow. Difficult encounters and adversity usually can be a type of learning, inspiring change. Throughout my life I have tried hard not to let disappointment get me down. I put negativity behind me as quickly as possible and focus on improvements.

I work hard and enthusiastically enjoy what I do. I try to be strong and alert and have self-control. I am assertive and not afraid to fail. I master whatever skills are necessary so that I can do my work properly and quickly. I am a team player and am considerate of others by practicing friendship, loyalty, and cooperation. I am not afraid to give praise and have confidence. I try to be myself and believe in myself at all times. And I love a challenge. Above all, I have faith and trust that things will work out as they should if I've done everything in my program. Last but not least, I practice patience: Good things take time.

I have been blessed with a good sense of self, which always allows me to continue whenever something or someone tries to beat me down. What also has helped to balance things out are the people who believe in me. You have to cherish those people, the people who believe in you. They are like the roots that firmly anchor a graceful willow tree in the eye of a storm.

And just as people have stood by me, I, too, have tried to help those I love focus on their own self-worth and believe in themselves. I have seen what happens when someone isn't given a chance or is criticized for trying.

Criticism, even when you try to ignore it, can hurt. I have cried over many articles written about me, but I move on and I don't hold on to that. Instead of giving in to pain inflicted by someone else, I focus on all the positive things in my life.

Someone once said to me, "You don't have a wrinkle on your face." And I said, "Not yet, but that's because I don't hold on to anger or disappointment. I just let all of that stuff go."

And that's what has helped me not to have any guilt or regrets today about leaving the Supremes, or getting a divorce, or anything else I ever have been criticized for doing in my life.

I guess it's also called peace of mind. When you have done your best and what you thought was right, then you can live with yourself and others.

I don't dwell on what might have been, and I don't let the past affect me. What I want in life is to live my vision and to fulfill my purpose on earth, to learn to master life and to pursue happiness.

These are the things I have learned, and I always try to follow them:

1. Be true to yourself.
2. Help others.
3. Make each day your masterpiece.

4. Drink deeply from good books (learn from all).
5. Build a shelter against a rainy day.
6. Make friendship a fine art.
7. Give thanks for your blessings.
8. Pray for guidance every day.

I also try to be unselfish, control my temper, and not use profanity. And never, ever, do I allow adversity or someone else's negativity stop me. I try to keep balanced, emotionally and physically, in everything I do. And I try to keep things in perspective: I don't aim too high, and I don't aim too low.

Abraham Lincoln once said that the worst thing you can do for those you love are the things they could and should do for themselves. I try to apply that principle in my life.

Full Circle

I gaze at myself
and see my womanhood
from the inside out

The core is strong, surrounded by
a web of feelings and desires

I'm certain of who I am —
I have been talking to myself for years.

I am at peace.

I am a Sparrow.

I am Diana

I am woman.

This is an important time for women. We are ushering in a new century with more power and opportunities than we have ever had in the history of the world. Doors are opening, but some of them still require a harder push. Women have become an important influence in the world, thanks in part to the many women over the centuries who

OPPOSITE PAGE:
Closing one door, another one opens.

have suffered, made sacrifices, and given their lives so that today we might enjoy certain freedoms and opportunities.

Although I am proud of what I have achieved in my life, there is a part of me that remains restless and uneasy, knowing there is still more to be done. I am filled with a quiet determination to accomplish my future goals. I feel that it is time to make a commitment to myself both as a woman and a free human being.

I enjoy simple things, like taking walks and looking at the world, the trees, the sky, all of nature. I want to listen to the birds, feel the wind, and smell the flowers. I want to be relaxed, to surrender into life. I like living in the moment, being in the "now." There are times, though, when I must think a year or two ahead and set goals. I guess I have been forced to do this because of the business in which I have always worked. In the entertainment business, you have to plan ahead in order to set up tours, reserve concert halls, and book time in a studio to record an album.

At this time in my life, setting goals so far ahead often means I have to keep working toward those goals, rather than using the time to savor the many wonders of life, to enjoy the people I love and who love me. I want to enjoy my life. My three young daughters and my two sons bring a youthful energy to my days. My children will never allow me to be old-fashioned, and I like that. It's important to me to keep up with what's going on. Being in the music business also helps me keep a youthful spirit because I mix with a lot of younger people. I stay fairly fit, too. I'm very active, and I still love to dance.

Because of the way my life is set up, a great deal is expected from me. I could feel this as a burden, but instead, I prefer to view my responsibilities and public image as a "push" that forces me gently to grow and better myself. There are ways of dealing with the world so that I invite the energy.

I am excited by the things I don't know. Life for me is a learning spree. It is my choice to make a difference in this world. Many of the problems our society faces don't have to exist, but attitudes like hatred and prejudice start with us.

I do my best to be fair and do the right thing. I also try to embrace change and not be afraid. Change is an essential part of life. If we take

risks and stay loving, we can give birth to new ideas and a new self, regardless of circumstances. If we learn to trust our inner voices, truth can come in a flash, although more often it unfolds over time, spiraling onward and upward, always moving. Life is change, and to resist change is to resist life.

I try to surrender and flow because the essence of life is a journey. The quality of that journey depends on each individual. It is up to each of us to take control of our lives and make the journey a sweet and valuable one.

The events, conditions, and experiences of our lives mold and shape us, often pushing us around like pieces on a giant chessboard. Life is the process of moving forward, sometimes stumbling, sometimes soaring. I have discovered that life is not the arrival at a particular destination but the journey itself, the odyssey.

> Life is a challenge.
> it is a plan
>
> listen
> and there is balance in our lives
> and quiet time.

239

As a woman, I know that I must take responsibility for everything that goes on in my life. I try not to allow myself to be a victim of either an abusive society or abusive men. As terrible as physical abuse may be, mental or emotional cruelty can be just as damaging. I am referring to the kind of manipulative behavior that causes low self-esteem by tapping into women's vulnerabilities and preying upon insecurities.

When I finally took charge of my life, my vision expanded. I understood the possibilities for me as a woman. I also knew I would have to face racism and sexism, a tough price to pay. But I continue to press forward, as we all must if we are to survive and progress. I try to seize all opportunities that come my way and make the best use of them. I keep my focus high. I have certain standards in my life and in my business. I have a way that works for me. I demand perfection from myself and the best possible job from all those around me. I wear a spiritual armor that strengthens me and helps me survive and endure this world. Otherwise, I would become too vulnerable and self-doubting and might submit to the negative forces that can sneak up from behind and try to jump me. A positive source of energy for me is the memory of my mother. She was my personal hero. There is so much she taught me. She prepared me for womanhood. The space that she once occupied in my heart and my life will always be there.

I am at a midpoint in my life. The loss of my mother, the ache, is something we are never prepared to accept. But I now occupy that same loving place inside the hearts of my own five children. The responsibility is mine. I have grown up, and it's my turn to guide them along their journey into the light. The more I live, the more energy I feel and the clearer I am about what I want to accomplish. Ageless beauty is a reflection of energy and love. I am convinced that this grows, not diminishes, with time.

Weaving the Tapestry

A Private Life

This wonderful gift of being a celebrity
carries a heavy burden
problems
intrusions
becoming a thing to overcome for my children.

My career has pushed me out into the public life. I enjoy it very much and try to handle it with grace. I want to be the kind of public figure that people respect. At the same time, my privacy is very important to me. I have mentioned the burden of being a person who is recognizable and the difficulties that public recognition raise, especially with my children. I have often thought how hard it must be for children to hold their mother as a precious gift in their lives when they must first overcome the fame.

Children must have their own individuality and independence. It is sometimes a difficult task. I remember when my oldest daughter, Rhonda, was much younger and used to go away to summer camp. I missed her very much and she didn't want me to visit, because I attracted

OPPOSITE PAGE:
I have the most wonderful relationships with my daughters.
We're best friends.

OVERLEAF:
There is no way I could have chosen a career over
my family and children.

too much attention, but I knew it was important for her to go. Today, we have a relationship in which she can talk to me about anything and tell me about her feelings. She's never held things inside.

My relationship and friendship with my girls is very true and honest. We have a bond that will always hold us together.

December 25, 1988

Dear Mommy,

Every day I learn something new about myself. It's a scary wonderful time. So many platforms I thought were solid concrete fall to ashes beneath my every step and knock me off balance. I'm looking forward with wonder and amazement to what lies ahead. Slowly, very slowly I'm learning what will be my life, what I can depend on and trust. Slowly I'm learning where to step.

With everything I learn about me, I begin to see others differently. I see them as people—not as moms, daddys. There are too many sisters and aunts and uncles in this world, but never enough individual people. This is what I'm learning.

I see you from a different perspective too now. I love our talks. They create a new dimension of the mother-daughter relationship—one where we are both people in every sense of the word. We fight with clenched teeth and fists and laugh until tears and we hug and know that we are safe. (That is my favorite part.)

I love what is becoming of our love. It's a bond that will only strengthen through my time at college—and strengthen too when we are together.

We need, still, to talk more. There are always so many things I'm thinking and learning and I feel I need to share them. I know there are things you hold inside. You can tell me. I am your most confidential friend.

You will never lose your daughter. It will be the one place that is always secure to place your foot, head or heart. Don't hesitate to step.

I love you,
Rhonda

I tried to teach my girls to talk about their feelings, not to hold on to anger or upset. If I do something they don't like, my children will tell me, "Mom, I didn't like it when you did that," or "Mom, I really don't want you to come to my class because it's very important that people recognize me and care about me for who I am. Not because I am Diana Ross's daughter."

I am mature enough to understand that, but sometimes it causes me great sadness because I want to share more in their lives. This is what I meant by "the burden of celebrity." When I walk into the gym to watch them do gymnastics or play basketball, the attention in the room gets directed at me. That is bothersome not only to me but also to the girls. We try to be sensitive to each other, to work it all out. I think we have done a pretty good job.

March 26, 1989

Dear Mommy,

I want to thank you for being you because without you I wouldn't be half the person that I am. You have given me your beauty and your wisdom among other things (your butt) and I love you with all my might. So I celebrate this day of your birth b/c I love you and respect you and look up to you. You are wonderful.

Love Always,
Your Second Daughter
Tracee

I'm proud of how I raised Rhonda, Tracee, and Chudney, and I am even more proud of who they have become, the integrity, honesty, and strength of character they each have developed.

I am so glad I had my children. Since I came from a large family, I always loved kids and wanted lots of my own. I had many girlfriends who decided they were going to work on their careers and have babies later in life. Then later got later and they didn't have any children. I was very picky about the projects I took so my work would not interfere with having children. That's one thing I will never regret: having my babies. I could not have gone this far in my career and returned home to an empty house. I am more a mother than a celebrity.

March 26, 1988

Dear Ms. Mommy,

Have a happy, happy, wonderful, great, fantastic, brilliant, super-duper, good, awsome, amazing, exciting, mind boggling, exhilarating, illuminating, delicious, cool, neat, totally wizard, splendid, pretty, handsome, superb, nice, sweet, bright, delightful, ecstatic, popping, amusing, hilarious, enlightening, peachy, interesting, time consuming, rosy, happening, rich, full, bright, miraculous, playful, enjoyable, fun filled, mystifying, birthday.

I love you so, so, so, so, so, so, so, so, so, so, so, so, so, so, so, so, so, so, so, so, so, so, so, so, so, so, so, so, so, so, so much and from here to the furthest unknown small out of the way galaxy,

Love,
Chudney #3 #6

Sorry no gift
couldn't get because
of Avalanche danger
Sorry sorry sorry
postponed till Monday
Please Please Please

Seal
of
Approval

For me, being a working mother is a blessing. I think my career was a positive force in raising my three daughters. I like to think it made me a better mother because since I was satisfied in my own life, I could encourage them to follow their personal destinies. I also think I was a positive role model in showing them how to balance commitments between work and family. I am extremely proud of all three of my daughters: Rhonda graduated from college in 1993 with honors, Tracee is doing well and graduates next year, and Chudney has just begun her freshman year in university. I love what Tracee wrote as she reflected on our relationship before her graduation from high school. I want to share some of it with you because it's wonderful and so is she:

The music starts, the curtain parts, and lights move. They hear her voice but where is she? Then the spotlight catches her on the right side, the left, the back of the room, or the top of the stage and she appears. Her beauty, talent and sincerity captures the audiences as she sings a song filled with meaning. That same woman has been there to send me off to school and to greet me when I get home, depending on the schedule. I heard Katharine Hepburn say that "women can't do it all," that "they have to choose between family and a career." Mom proved that wrong. She has a successful career and strong family. She does it all and everyone stays happy. People are influenced by her music, they idolize her as an entertainer, black successful woman in motherhood and business and as a person. I see her as all those things but from a different perspective because she is my mother.

She has been both mother and father to me and my two sisters. She is away a lot whether for a night or a month but she calls whenever she can. We have a different home life than most. We are always figuring out the logistics so that we can all be together. But despite all that she has created a strong foundation on which our family is based. She is determined, confident, motivated . . . by a good heart and so many other things. She has taken all of those things and built a family from them with morals and ideals. . . .

My mother also created a successful career from nothing except talent and self-motivation. She is an entertainer who takes care of all her own business and is loved by her audiences. She creates projects, goals and dreams and she tries to achieve them. Whether the dream is to one day sing in Central Park or to clean out the closet on the third floor, there is always something new to tackle. For her, as she sings, "There ain't no mountain high enough." She believes that having dreams is what keeps us happy. There is a song she sings about that. The line says, "dreams see us through to forever" which reflects a part of Mom. At the end of the song she says, "hold on to your dreams." That's a strange time in a concert because she is talking to the audience on one level and me on another. I hear that coming from my mother. It makes it stronger. It is real motivation because I know that's what she does. I know it's possible for dreams to become reality. Others might listen to that and say, "It may have worked for her but I'm nothing like her." Or, "How do I know it's true?" Since she is my mother and I know that it is true, I know it is possible that I can do it, too.

She tells me to go for my dreams with all that I've got but to remember that if I don't succeed because of obstacles or anything else "it's not the end of the world. Follow a new path. Change directions. Try something else." I gathered from watching her that it's not the arrival it's the journey. It's the pursuit of happiness, the hard hike up to the top that makes you enjoy it when you get there. Sometimes you have to take risks. You have to put your foot where it might slip or you won't get to the summit. She says, "It's the difficult things that make you appreciate the good ones. If everything was perfect then it wouldn't be perfect it would just be."

She is a role model for me, a motivation. I see mirrored in her career the philosophies that she passes to me at home and I realize that it is possible to start on my own and build on a dream to reach a goal. I can get to my summit, too. I can do it and I will. I'll go for my dreams and goals. And you better watch out because "I'm Coming Out" (another song of hers) of high school and I am moving into the world.

I share these private moments with you to let you know how important it is for me, as a celebrity, to still have a private life.

Dear
Ms. Mommy,

Have a happy, happy,
wonderful, great, fantastic,
brilliant, superduper, good,
awsume, amazing, exiting, mind
boggling, exilerating, olimlining,
delicios, cool, neat, totaly wizard,
splendid, pretty, hansome, superb,
nice, swell, bright, delightful, extatic,
popping, amusing, hilarios, lightning,
peachy, intresting, sweet, loud,
time consuming, rosey exapeening,
rich, full, bright, meraculous,
playful, enjoyable, fun filled,
on mystyfying, birthday.

I love you so, so, so,
so, so, so, so, so, so,
so, so, so, so, so, so, so,
so, so, so, so, so, so, so, so,
so, so, so, so, so, so, so, so, so,
so, so, so, so, so, so much
and from here-to the furthest
unknown, small outof the way
galaxy, small outof the way

Love Chudan #3 #6

March 26, 89

Dear mommy,

I want to thank you for being
you b/c without you I wouldn't
be half the person that I am. You
have given me your beauty & your
wisdom among other things (your
butt) and i love you with all my might.
So i celebrate this day of your birth
b/c I love you and, respect you
and look up to you. You are
wonderful.

Love Always,
your second daughter.
Tracie

December 25, 1989

Dear Mommy,

Everyday I learn something
new about myself. It's a scary
wonderful time. So many old forms
I thought were solid crumble fell
to ashes beneath my every
step and throw me off balance
I'm teeting toward with wonder
and amazement to what lies
ahead. Slowly, very slowly I'm
learn what will be my life, what
I can depend on and trust. Slowly,
I'm learning where to step.

With everything I learn about
me, I begin to see others differently
— I see them as people — not as
mommys & daddys. There are too
many sisters and aunts and
uncles in this world, but never
enough individual people — this is
what I'm learning.

I see you from a different
perspective too now. I love our
talks. They create a new dimension

of the mother-daughter relationship
— one where we are both people in
every sense of the word. We hurt
with clentched teeth and fists
and laugh until tears and we hug &
know (that we are safe (that is
my favorite part.)

I love what is becoming of
our love. It's a bond that will
only strenghten through my time
at college — and strengthen too
when we are together.

We need, still, to talk more
there are always so many things
I'm thinking and learning and
I feel I need to share them.
I know there are things you hold
inside — You can tell me. I
am your most confidential
friend.

You will never lose your daughter.
I will be the one place that is
always secure to place your
foot, heart. Don't
hesitate to step

I love you
Rhonda

Sorry NO Gift
couldn't get because
of Avalanch danger
Sorry sorry sorry
Posponed till Monday
Please Please Please

Seal
OF
Approval

Goose Bumps

London

October 9, 1986

My dear girl,

For me there is pleasure in a roaring storm.
For me there is pleasure to fight and win.
For me there is pleasure in boldness and risk.
For me there is pleasure in doing what others dare not to do.

But this I have had, this I have done.
You hold a promise for a greater treasure something
only you can give. With you I hope to discover
brighter skies, milder suns and seas peaceful to the
soul that seeks them.

For you I will capture the brightest star.

I love you,
Arne

S ome of my most electrical and life-altering experiences have happened in the rain: the performance in Central Park and the first time I met my husband. By the way, I was not looking for a husband when I

OPPOSITE PAGE:
With love, all things are possible.

met Arne. I do think that this is when it happens; when you're not out looking, they sort of find you.

Arne is a businessman in the deepest sense. To hear him speak about our meeting sounds quite factual. To me, it was an exquisite scene from a movie: romance, passion, sparks, and lightning. They say that truth is always more interesting than fiction could ever be. In this case, it was certainly so.

Setting: The scene opens in Nassau, a perfect tropical island for man-meets-woman. I had been touring, and I needed to spend some time with my kids. It was to be a short trip, a little swimming in the day and lots of sleeping in the night, a great way to rest, unwind, and be with my girls. My girlfriend Joanne came with me for companionship. The thought never crossed my mind that fate might have something very powerful in store. Isn't that always the way?

Weather conditions: Rain, rain, and more rain. I was, needless to say, a little bit disappointed. Arne Naess, a Norwegian shipping magnate living in London, had just returned from climbing Mount Everest, a worthy adventure for the hero in any story. He also wanted to be with his kids, so from opposite sides of the world we two converged in this rain-drenched paradise.

The scene opens around a swimming pool, rain pouring down, the kids playing in the pool, oblivious to the weather. Splashing around, they instantly make friends with a few other children. Mine are too young to be alone, so I have to be there watching. Wearing a big red hat to keep the rain off my face, I drag a chair under a small balcony and sit beneath it. I stay there, slightly bored and detached, watching my kids, and suddenly there is a man walking toward me. I don't even look up, knowing he will sit beside me as there is no other place to find shelter from the rain. He moves another chair under the balcony and quietly sits. I realize that the other children are his. As he seems intent on watching the children, I get up and return to my bungalow. I don't even see his face.

The scene shifts. The six children end up at my bungalow, sitting on the floor, playing monopoly. This is normal; I have always been a magnet for children. So here we all are in Nassau, on a supposedly sunshiny vacation, stuck inside all day. The kids, of course, are unconcerned about the weather. They are one boy and five girls, and they are all getting along famously.

Suddenly the first miracle happens—the sun pushes its way through the dense cloud covering and emerges. Warmth and light enter the scene and Nassau begins to resemble the tropical paradise depicted in the travel brochures. The kids rush out to the beach with Joanne. I enjoy the quiet solitude for a short while and then go out to join them. I never make it there. As I walk toward the beach, they are already walking back. The man from under the balcony is walking with them, and for the first time I see his face. I like what I see.

"You have been with the children most of the day," he says to me. "Why don't I take them out to dinner?"

"Okay. Fine," I say. That sounds good to me. Joanne and I want to go out gambling tonight and now we can.

When destiny has something in store, it uses all available tools to achieve its end. The rains come once again. They pour down in rivers upon the land, and I watch my children dress to go out to dinner with another family. Perhaps I am prompted by unseen forces. I suddenly know exactly what I want to do. I say to Tracee, "Joanne and I have decided not to go out gambling. It's raining too hard. Would you ask the gentleman if we could also join him for dinner?"

The answer is yes.

Another shift in the action, a new scene.

I let them go on to dinner without me. I will meet them soon. I start dressing, I think I must have been on the phone for a little while. Just before I leave, I realize that the dress I have chosen has a long row of tiny buttons all the way down the back. I can't button them by myself. Oh well, no bother, I'll let Tracee do it for me as soon as I get there.

New setting: I jump into a little go-cart and arrive at the private club in Layford Cay, so beautiful, the perfect spot for the climax of the scene. I walk in the door looking for Tracee and Arne jumps up. He instantly charms me; he is wearing a bow tie that I adore. He comes over to greet me. I smile.

"Oh, you didn't have to wait for me," I say. "You guys could have started. I was just going to join you."

He smiles and motions that it's okay, he doesn't mind. I hang back a

253

moment and then say to him with a little blush, "I can't button my dress. Could you ask my daughter Tracee to come out and help me?"

Without hesitation, he says, quite matter-of-factly, "I'll do it." Three little words. I don't know why I am allowing this, but before I know it, I am turning around, piling my hair on top of my head with my hands, and a stranger is buttoning my dress. He starts at the top. As he clumsily tries to do up the tiny buttons with his big hands, I realize that the buttons go clear down to my bottom. He reaches the middle of my back very slowly, he is having trouble with the size of the buttons, and my flesh is beginning to stand out in goose bumps. I feel strange now. "It's really all right," I tell him. "I can have Tracee do the rest." But this is a man who has just climbed Mount Everest. He is no quitter. He makes his way all the way down. He is finally finished, I let loose my hair, and we walk in to dinner together.

Another perfect set: He has taken a large round table in the center of the floor of this most elegant dining room. As I approach the table, the seating arrangement, which I expect happened randomly, seems to suggest a strange pattern. Beneath beautiful crystal chandeliers, Joanne, Arne, and the bigger girls are grouped together, almost according to age, the smaller girls come next, giggling amongst themselves, and then, finally, the boy, Christoffer.

Arne seats me beside him, we begin to talk, and then suddenly the special effects begin. The entire scene around me fades out. Seating patterns, giggling girls, waiters, all float weightlessly in the air around us. The scene is now a two-shot. Arne and I. I am completely fascinated with Arne Naess, the man who has just climbed Mount Everest, the man who in doing so has just peeled off a layer of his skin. He speaks openly and honestly while we eat a beautiful dinner and sip white wine.

Suddenly, the rest of the world rematerializes. Dinner is apparently over and the kids are saying, "Let's go." As I float out of the restaurant, still caught in the enchantment, it occurs to me that he knows nothing of my career or who I am. His daughter has said to him, "Don't you know who this is? It's Diana Ross." He thinks he remembers seeing me perform somewhere, but he really isn't sure. I think he has seen me a long time ago with the Supremes, but never on my own.

The magic isn't over. The next morning, before he leaves, he and his kids stop over to say good-bye. He is wearing khaki pants and a khaki shirt. He has brought a camera, and we all pose for Polaroid pictures. Now comes miracle number 2. First, he stands with all the kids, and then I do. When we look at the pictures, they look like family groupings. Eerie. We exchange numbers. I tell him, "If you are ever in New York, please call me." He says, "If you are ever in London, do the same." I still have the vision of him walking away and saying to myself, "I'm going to see this guy again." I keep my photograph. In fact, I still have it.

There the scene ended, but the energy did not. A short time later, the exact timing escapes me, I received a phone call. It was from Arne. "I will be passing through New York City on my way to California. I just wondered what your plans are because maybe we can have lunch or dinner or something." I was also going to L.A. We could meet there. Excited, I agreed to dinner.

255

We went to Jimmy's. We were having a pleasant enough conversation about who he was and who I was, the regular "getting to know you" stuff, when he suddenly took his finger and brushed it lightly across the skin of my hand. Just a gentle touch but one of the most sexual sensations I have ever had. Startled, I yanked my hand away and gasped, "Why did you do that? Why did you do that?" I repeated myself because I was so nervous. We had been in the most innocent conversation, and the sudden departure from the normalcy into the sensuality had taken me by surprise. Perhaps it was a surprise for him, too.

When dinner was finished, we decided to go out dancing, but first there was something I wanted to do. I had to introduce Arne to my best friend, Suzanne de Passe. It was very late, but I tried to call her anyway. There was no answer. So we passed by her house and I awakened her from a sound sleep. She was obviously not in a position to receive visitors. The introduction would have to wait. Arne and I went to a disco and danced for hours.

When the evening was about to end, he told me, "I have to fly to New York, but I want to come back to California to see you again."

Again, he surprised me. "You mean you're going all the way to New York and then you want to fly all the way back here?" I asked in disbelief.

"Yes, if we can have dinner tomorrow night."

You know what the answer was. We married soon after that. We both shared the feeling of wanting to get on with the rest of our lives. We didn't have time for courting and all the rest of it. We just went for it.

About a month after our marriage, I went to Norway to visit him. He had broken a rib. He never spoke about his pain, that's the kind of man he is. I wouldn't have even known about it if I hadn't caught him once trying to hang on to the side of the door, shaking his ribs into place. Even though we were married, I never felt I knew much about him then because it has never been his way to talk much about himself.

I remember shortly after the Nassau trip, I was having lunch with a girlfriend and I told her that I had met this very good-looking man. She asked me, "Don't you know who that family is?" I shook my head; he had told me nothing about that. Several days later, she sent me a couple of books about the Naess family. Through those books, I learned that one of Arne's uncles is in the shipping business and Arne had followed in his footsteps. The other uncle, who shares Arne's name, is a philosopher, and it turns out that I have grown quite close to him. I enjoy conversing with him and find him to be a very nice man.

Arne is a scruffy guy. He is a natural man and likes to be comfortable. Despite our differences, we get along very well, but the living situation is a strain. He tried to get his business started here with me, but it was too difficult. His business moved to London, and he went with it. I really don't think he expected me to follow.

I love Arne very much and we have the two boys, but I also have my girls. Rhonda is twenty-one, has her own apartment, and is settled into her own life. She has just graduated from college, and Chudney is just beginning college. Tracee has one more year before she graduates. I can't abandon one family for another. Arne understands this. He feels the same about his children. We both travel a lot and that makes it hard on us, but I would find it hard just to sit at home waiting for my husband to arrive to take me out to dinner.

In my life, I need things to do and I need a purpose. I have to have something to get up for in the morning. I am not well connected in London; I don't have many friends. Although I know I can create a life, I would find it difficult at this time to let go of my life here at home to move to Europe. Of course I want to be with my husband and he wants to be with me, and when we feel that, those are the difficult times. I know that it is also hard on the boys because they really need their father.

Somehow, we have managed to work it out. I think that we love each other so much that love gets us through everything. And the time apart keeps the romance alive. When he has been away, it feels like it's all brand-new and we really look forward to being with each other. Our evenings together are spontaneous and passionate. It all ends up being very wonderful, but living like this is becoming more and more difficult. We'll see what the future brings.

June 10, 1988

Dearest Arne,

Thank you for sharing that experience with me. It's as if I were there with you watching you from some distant place.

I envy your love for the climb. I know not to worry about you. It's really so wonderful that you have this special feeling when you climb—it's yours and yours alone.

I'm sitting alone in the kitchen since 5:45 having coffee, missing you. Until I see you on Tuesday, I'm counting the days.

How are you feeling now? Are you well? Is your stomach better?

Ross is still asleep. He's really growing full of vitality—eager to walk and get around. Hurry and see him, my love. Each of these moments are so precious.

I feel like a drag—I'm not very happy these days. But I'm really fighting it the best I know how.

I love and miss you too.

Your wife
(lonely for you)

Arne and I have been married for seven years now, and because of the flexibility of our arrangement, we have both been able to make the adjustment. I feel that couples should not collapse into a marriage. You don't have to lose your identity or any part of yourself. When each person brings one hundred percent into a relationship, the merging of those two people should give you two hundred percent, nothing lost, much gained. That's true synergy.

Of course there is the pain of separation. I got used to being alone and deciding everything for myself when I was a single parent for nine years. I don't want to get used to Arne's not being there. I want to be able to say, "Somebody help me button my dress." A companion is someone with whom you can bounce things off. When I don't have that, when Arne is gone for long periods of time, I feel too alone.

I'm thinking about moving to London in the future because I would like to travel less than I do now. I always want to sing, but I'd also like to write more, particularly children's books and inspirational material. I feel that I have something to say, and that's a way I could keep working and be closer to my husband and children whom I love so very much.

Until it all gets worked out, deep down in my heart I know that no matter where we are, Arne loves me and is always close. And if I ever forget, I have his letters to remind me. I'd like to share just a bit of one of his letters with you, one that he wrote when he was far away, high up in the mountains.

> *My girl,*
>
> *I am not ever away from you. You are always with me especially here among the mountains.*
>
> *The taste of your kiss, the smell of your skin, the excitement of our lovemaking, all linger with me to build my dream of you on. When alone my imagination takes you with me over the blossoms of Alpine meadows to the highest peaks. As I wander alone you are my companion, when I lay down amongst the flowers you lay with me and my desire for you my girl is as strong and wild as ever.*
>
> *Your man*

I   Mountains
                 April 29th.

My girl,
I am not ever away
from you — you are
always with me
especially here among
the mountains.

The memory of your kiss,
the smell of your skin,
the excitement of our
lovemaking all linger
with me to build my
dream of you on.

II

When alone my
imagination takes
you with me over
the blossoms of alpine
meadows to the
highest peaks. As I
wonder alone you
are my companion,
when I lay down
amongst the flowers
you lay with me
and my desire for
you my girl is as
strong and wild as
ever.
            Your man.

Antique Lace

Arne and I got married in Lausanne, Switzerland, although not in the original location we wanted. We used to pass by a beautiful castle in Chillon along the drive to our chalet from Geneva. It was a historical, magical place, and I remember saying to Arne, "I would love to get married there." He told me, "Well, why don't we see if they have special occasions there. Maybe we can use it." We finally had to abandon the idea, but only after extensive checking and trying all kinds of ways to make it possible. That's what I love about Arne, his sense of romance and his attempts to do things in a special way and to make every moment count.

When I realized that I could not get the castle in Chillon, I searched for a small church all around the same area in Geneva. I finally found a lovely old abbey in Lausanne with which I was very happy. It seemed that once we had decided on the place, everything else, like preparing the invitations and finding the florist, happened magically. I met a wonderful American woman living in Geneva who helped me plan the entire day. When I performed at Radio City Music Hall, there was a sweet baker who used to make me a special cake each night. I found him and commissioned him to make the wedding cake, a magnificent creation covered in jewels.

Elizabeth Courtney makes the most beautiful gowns, so I couldn't imagine choosing anyone else to make my wedding gown. Over the previous five years, although I had no knowledge that I would be getting married, I had been collecting antique lace. That's one of the

OPPOSITE PAGE:
My wedding was everything I had hoped it would be –
the answer to my dreams.

things I like to do. I had my gown made from this beautiful lace. I wanted to wear white, but it is said that in a second marriage you're not supposed to. I compromised with an eggshell cream color, and I wore a tiny diamond tiara that I had bought in Paris. It was old and delicate, a perfect match to the lace in the dress.

There was so much work: the sending of the invitations, the seating at the reception, the planning of the meal. It was all worth it, it was so very memorable. I shall never forget the details of how we found the different flowers, the gowns for each of the girls, Rhonda, Tracee, Chudney, and Arne's two girls, Katinka and Leona. The gowns were all peach, but each one was different and lovely. We had someone wonderful come by to style and put flowers in our hair.

On the day of the wedding, when Suzanne, my maid of honor, arrived, she took over. She took charge of overseeing everything so that I had a chance to gather myself. She allowed me to be a guest at my own wedding.

I wanted a big wedding because I didn't have that when I married the first time. Bob and I had eloped; we had quickly gone to Las Vegas and were married in a small chapel there. It had held its own kind of magic, but I had always dreamed of a large wedding, one to which I could invite all the friends, family, and loved ones of both my husband and myself. Unfortunately, it was too far for all of my American friends to attend, but Steve Wynn flew over some of them in his plane, including Gregory Peck and his daughter.

Suzanne was the ring bearer, and I will never forget the joke that Arne played on her. During the ceremony, she dropped the ring on the floor and she couldn't find it. One look at her face told me that she was beginning to panic, but Arne had actually picked it up and wasn't letting on that he had it. After much anxiety, she finally realized what was happening. She handled his teasing very well. When people got up to speak at the reception, she was in tears because she was so happy for me. Suzanne is one of my sweetest, dearest friends.

Arne was able to get the Norwegian Boys Choir to sing at our wedding. They walked into the church holding candles, and their voices sounded as if they had come straight from heaven. I invited my American minister, Wintley Phipps. He sang a song that he had written especially for us. When I try to think of words to describe the feelings of that day, I think of heavenly, magical, romantic, godlike, blessed. We felt so very blessed.

Arne and I were moved by the blending of our friends and families. Both of our parents were there. My father was so very proud of me, not that I was marrying Arne but simply proud of the things that I had accomplished in my life. It made him feel good about himself.

After the wedding, we went on a honeymoon to Tahiti; Arne owns an island near there. It's very small but completely private, and we were like Adam and Eve, running around naked. All I can say is we were very, very happy.

The experience of my wedding was everything I had hoped it would be. It was the beginning of the magic that still runs through my marriage today. It was the answer to my dream, so beautiful and special that I am saving everything to give to my daughters for their weddings.

Thinking of a Rainbow

[Your children] come through you but not from you.
Kahlil Gibran, *The Prophet*

From the beginning of our marriage, Arne and I wanted to have a family together. Even though I knew it would be difficult being an older parent, even though it would be a great deal of responsibility for us at this time, I still wanted to have his child. That's a part of our relationship and the love I have for him.

When Ross was born, there was a twelve-year difference between Chudney and him. He would basically be growing up alone with older parents. I decided to have Evan because I wanted Ross to have a brother or sister. I didn't know if that would prove difficult at my age, but my mother had always said that raising two was just like raising one. I wanted Ross to have a friend, not to be an only child.

My two pregnancies were very close together, only ten months apart. I knew that I had to be very careful. As a parent in her forties, I had to take tests and examinations to make sure that the babies were healthy. I did all of the things I was supposed to do; I tried to eat right and to stay active. I actually gained a lot of weight with Evan because I had intense cravings for Häagen-Dazs ice cream, but I lost it again and we all turned out fine.

Childbirth and having babies are the most magical times for me. Children give such special meaning to my life, and I often wonder what it would have been like if I had never had any. When my boys are

OPPOSITE PAGE:
When I wrote my children's book, *When You Dream*, I wanted very much to create characters that deal with real-life things – not witches and fairies, but children's normal fears.

grown, I might have to adopt because I love having babies around. I know that when the music is gone, when no one remembers "Ain't No Mountain High Enough," my children will still be there. There was no way I could ever have chosen a career over my family and my children.

> My little child
> close your eyes
> think of a rainbow
> shining colors
>
> My babies
> I love you so
> my little children
> beautiful
> magic
> I love you forever
> I'll be there for you forever
> and always
> for you
>
> Evan was going off to sleep and he
> said "Mommy I'm thinking of a rainbow."
> suddenly Ross who I thought was asleep
> joined in.
> "Oooh," said Ross.
> I remember seeing one too.
> Mom, wasn't it beautiful
>
> My life has been a rainbow of beautiful colors
> but like a rainbow,
> the rain comes first
>
> The sun is shining
> don't run away
> stay there

be in the light
it'll be all right
floating on a dream
can you believe
try and believe

Beautiful babies
thank you for being
here in my life
thank you babies
nice – it's so nice

There's nothing I'd rather do
than be here
loving you
good night

Sometimes when my kids are asleep, I tiptoe into their room and just gaze at them. In these moments, I thank God for my life. I love my time at home, knowing that my kids are in the other room, playing or sleeping. When you have babies, you realize that all these little ones know of life is what they pick up from you, so I try to be a good example.

I work hard at being a good mother, and I feel that I am one. When they get older and I'm no longer around, I think they will remember that when they were sad or had a fever or cold, Mom was there. As I raise Ross and Evan, I do everything in my power to keep them intellectually challenged, culturally stimulated, and emotionally strong, happy young men. I try to teach them the Golden Rule as my parents gave it to me.

I teach them to respect others and to treat all people fairly. I let them know that they don't have to like everything about people to love them. My desire to be a positive role model for them is my inspiration to practice love in all the moments of my life, and I will try to live that way until the end of my life. I want to get my moment right, and I want my children to get their moments right.

I try to teach my kids about forgiveness. This is something we all need to learn. Holding grudges acts like a slow disease or a cancer that eats away at our souls. We must learn how to let go of anger and hate, to forgive others and ourselves. I try to learn from my mistakes and when someone has hurt me in my life, I try to remember to send love. These are the things that I hope my children will learn from watching me.

I have found thoughts and words to be the foundation for success and failure in life. I'm teaching my kids when to whisper and when to shout. Words often can hurt, especially between men and women. I want my children to understand how to use the power of words to bind them to others, not to divide them. I want my sons to have a healthy respect for women. I would like them to grow up knowing the joys of friendship and companionship between men and women and to know that husbands are not meant to be fathers to their wives but rather friends, lovers, buddies, and partners. I am confident that my sons will be strong in their values and a great source of pride for both Arne and me.

Although I'm a very light sleeper and can usually hear my children before they even get to my door, I always sleep with my door open so they can come in if they need me. The open-door policy is something Arne has had to get used to. When I am away, all of my children know they can phone me at any hour, any day, no matter where I am or what I am doing. No one on my staff or anyone else is allowed to stop them from getting to me. The boys don't yet understand why I sometimes have to be away overnight. When I'm on tour, we miss each other so much that I spend a lot of time flying back and forth, just for the joy of walking into their rooms in the middle of the night to cover them up and kiss them. Even if I have only slept a few hours, I wake up early, have breakfast with them, and see them off to school. I have found that the important thing is that I let the children know I am there.

The boys are four and five now, and it seems they are already turning into young men. I try to be there for all of their most important events, just as I have for my girls. Sometimes it's hard, but the joy of supporting them, in knowing they can see my face and know I am there, outweighs the discomfort. I try to make my schedules around their plays and their birthdays. I will not tour at those times unless there is no way around it. Everyone who works with me knows my children are my first priority, and if they have families, I feel the same about them. When I do it this way, when I know my children feel safe, secure, and happy, all areas of my life run much better.

My family is my team. It hasn't always been easy balancing the many roles and demands of being a working mother and wife, but the rewards are golden. I spend a lot of time thinking about my children. They are always in my mind and my heart, and I constantly say a prayer of protection that they be sheltered and taken care of in this universe.

I am well along in my personal quest of living my vision, of fulfilling my purpose on earth and learning to master life. My children are just beginning theirs. I want to share my life experience with them as much as possible. I would like them to become the best that they can be and to have a clear understanding of themselves. In this way, they may better understand the world.

I have learned the difference between
loneliness and being alone.

I am on the verge of something. Each day I can just feel it. Something special is about to happen. Expect a miracle today.

PREVIOUS SPREAD: I fight hard for my privacy. It is very important to keep balance in my life. Beauty is a reflection of energy and love that grows, not diminishes with time.

Snow Crystals

A rne and I are having lunch on a roof terrace in the Yak and Yeti
Hotel in Kathmandu. The air is crystal clear. In the distance we
can see the high mountains of the Himalayas, the abode of goddesses,
the home of the elusive yeti, and the birthplace of Buddha. We are about
to be helicoptered to Namche Bazar, the center of the Sherpa community. From there, we will walk toward Everest Base Camp.

I am here because of Arne. He wants me to see and feel this wondrous
place. I am so happy to be able to be a part of his world. The mountains
move him in ways that nothing else can, and I want to understand this
part of him. I wonder what these mountains will do to me, a girl from
Detroit, where there are no hills, let alone massive mountain ranges.

As we land in Namche Bazar, I feel dwarfed as I step out of the
helicopter and look around. The altitude is eleven thousand feet, and we
are standing on a hillside, surrounded by the most magnificent mountains I can ever imagine. Far in front of us, above all others, we can see
Mount Everest, Sagarmatha, the Goddess Mother of the Earth, as she is
called by those who live in the valley below. I think I understand the
name as I gaze at her plume, created by the jet stream that sweeps across
her summits, forming a banner of snow crystals, stretching far into
Tibet. I then gaze with equal wonder at Arne, standing beside me. In
this moment, he is my husband, a regular man of flesh and blood, but he
is also more than that. He seems godlike, as he has struggled and sweated
his way up that magnificent mountain. He has dug his feet into her ice

and snow, and step by step, in the biting cold, made his way up her treacherous sides and stood on the peak of this powerful goddess. He knows that kind of magic. The purpose of this trip is twofold. He wants to share his world with me, and he also wants to visit the community of Sherpas who accompanied him on his wondrous climb. A bond was created, and he has a need to reconnect and visit them from time to time.

The first night we stay in a small rugged-looking hut they call a "teahouse." There is no heating at all, but we have our double sleeping bags. Arne assures me that we will be warm as toast. I trust him with my life, but not with his assessment of whether or not I will freeze. On a normal summer's day, he complains bitterly about the unbearable heat. When it is freezing by just about anybody's standards, he calls it pleasantly brisk. He seems to think that heat is bad and cold is good. We have endless conversations on this subject. In the dead of winter, he opens the windows wide. In his apartment in London, he has no heating; he simply has no need for it. When the drinking water that I keep beside my bed is frozen in the morning, that's the kind of cold he likes. I like the heat.

On this particular trip, I quickly realize that Arne is going to have it his way. He doesn't even try to open the windows because it is unnecessary. The wind whips straight through the gaps in the walls and the roof. When I evaluate the situation, I know that tonight Arne will be happy. I try not to think about sleeping.

We are in a top-of-the-line teahouse. For dinner, they serve us potatoes, eggs, chapatis, and chang, the local beer, which is white as milk. After a hard day, I could have done with something more substantial. Since there is no electricity, we decide to go to bed at eight P.M. I change into a sexy silk nightgown. Arne looks at me and smiles. "You look devastating, but I think you will be happier in your baggy long johns." Of course he is right. Even in my warmest woollies, the night is long and cold, but I just shiver and stay silent. I am afraid to complain; it is only the first night.

The next day, we walk to Chunlungchi by way of Pangpoche. There we stay in another of these huts called teahouses beside a small river. As the several prayer wheels churn, a prayer is said over and over, "OM MANI PADME HUM." These same words, which are written on the many mani stones along the path, translate as "The jewel is in the heart of the Lotus flower." They tell me that the real meaning is deeply spiritual and only to be found in the depths of eternity and the silence of purity.

The Chunlungchi Teahouse consists of one all-purpose room, which serves as kitchen, living room, and bedroom. I am always cold. I especially dread the nights. I can't seem to get warm, no matter what I do.

When night falls, Arne and I sleep in one bed and the entire Sherpa family, mother, father, and two kids, sleep in the other. The children seem literally to live in that bed. When they return from school, which is a two-hour walk in each direction, they climb back on the bed to do their homework.

In the morning, we walk for hours and hours. It is never-ending, always uphill, until we reach Thyangboche. Located 13,500 feet above sea level, this is the world's highest monastery. Behind the monastery, I am impressed with the towering eminence of Ama Dablam. It is hard to believe, but at our new location, the view is even more spectacular than it was in Namche Bazar.

The weather is changing. Unfortunately for me, it keeps getting colder, much colder. Before bed, I put on every item of clothing I have brought with me, plus some of Arne's. I climb into my sleeping bag and I am still freezing. Arne piles everything he can find on top of me: rucksacks, raincoats. He jokes that he is covering me with everything that is not nailed down. I lie beneath my own private mountain and still I freeze. I will never understand how Arne and his climbing friends can take it in the snow, high on a mountaintop, forty degrees below zero, and actually like it.

The next day, after I climb out from under my clothing mountain, I see that the snow has fallen overnight. We are now in two feet of crystal powder. It is magnificently beautiful, but as unbelievable as it seems, even colder than yesterday. My memory of the trip is filled with hardy

273

and friendly people, the majesty of the mountains, the wonder of Buddhism, and the feeling of being always, always cold.

My husband, Arne, is a wonderful man who loves and admires my independence, as I do his. It is one of the things that first attracted us to each other. But it is this very same independence and commitment to our respective professions that sometimes intrudes on our relationship.

For the moment, we remain great jugglers as we struggle to balance our careers and family life. A good juggler tries to stay organized. I have to work very hard to make everything mesh, but I know that if anything in my life falls between the cracks, how I handled a situation all comes back to me. Perhaps I did not pay enough attention to some small detail. I try to stay aware so that I do not miss anything. I am especially attentive to anything that affects my children.

Arne has three wonderful children: Christoffer, Katinka, and Leona. When we married, I was surprised to find that being a stepmother was not as easy as I thought it would be. I take well to most kids and they usually like me, but I think that Arne's children had a normal reaction to the woman their father married. They must have felt that I was taking their father away from them. They loved Ross and Evan right away, but they found it very hard to accept me. Of late, now that Arne and I have been married for more than eight years, they have started being much more comfortable with me.

It's about respect. Respect takes time. It isn't something that is there when you first meet people. It has to be earned. It takes authentic caring about each other. Because I travel so much, they have not had the time to feel my heart and know who I really am.

I have always loved older people. When I was a young kid, I was a candy striper. I used to go to hospitals for the aged and hold their hands, brush their hair, even change bedpans. I didn't mind that. I have always been patient and understanding with older people, in much the same way that I am with children, so I loved meeting Arne's mother. She is a wonderful woman, and I am excited about having her in my life. I cherish her wisdom, and while I am sad that the boys never knew my

mother, I am so happy that they get to have one wonderful grandmother.

I face my marriage with the same positive attitude with which I try to
face all situations in my life. I feel the challenges that are in front of me. I
have dealt with the past, and I am excited about the future. I want to live
each day completely.

> It's hard to love a great man.
> it's hard to intimately love
> or truly have togetherness
> with a great man.
> There is always that distance,
> that mystery,
> that place that you don't touch,
> that place that you can't get to.

275

With love, all things are possible.

Miracles

As I look back
each step in my life
was necessary and complete
and perfect.

Looking at my Tapestry of Life,
the weaving of its threads
the colors of the yarn,
the textures, its flow and feel
gives it its uniqueness
that speaks only to me.

If I touch it, it feels
rough, soft, smooth, ups and downs,
filled with lessons and decisions.
The streets and apartments
I grew up in.
the voice that led me on my travels,
and people and friends,
my children
and lovers,
tightly woven in my cloth.

My travels lead me to where I am today.
sometimes these steps have felt

OPPOSITE PAGE:
The only way I can thank you is to be the best that I can be.

painful, difficult,
but led me to greater
happiness and opportunities.

I've learned through my pain and struggles,
by writing these memoirs,
and by remembering.
I see that these were lessons
of great importance.

I know now that all these changes
were probably meant to be its design.
my special pattern.
I realize I have learned
from all my moments.

Through it all, there has always been music.

My purpose in life
has been clear to me for a long time now.
it may change.
I know I'm here to serve
and to help others,
children in particular,
and make a difference in the world.

I've chosen these paths,
or have they chosen me?

"The secret is, there is no secret."

Diana

I am on the verge of something new. Each day I can just feel it. I know something special is about to happen.

I have spent the last year of my life looking back, remembering. Time has passed quickly, and the process has been magical, wonderful. When I was in it, it often felt like a painful struggle. When things happen, they are sometimes difficult to understand, especially when there is pain involved. But I believe that everything has a purpose, that everything that comes into our lives is perfect.

There has been a great deal of richness in my life; it has been very full. I have always seen myself as a passionate, private person. I try to focus on the good things. I appreciate the beauty in life. I am reminded of how lucky I am, and I thank God constantly. I hunger for more knowledge, for the opportunity to learn new and different things. I try to push beyond my comfort zones, experiencing all that is new, forever taking the challenge. I hope that my experiences serve as an inspiration for each of you to reach for your dreams as I have reached for mine.

I don't feel I am very complicated, but I am really happy to have the gift to be able to enjoy my life, even as I face my fears. I see more clearly each day, and I try to inspire others and to make a difference through my example.

Looking back through my life, I see that I am not really angry about anything. There have been many turning points and peak experiences. I have learned a lot about myself, and I know there is so much more. My personal spiritual search has reached new heights. It is my intent to find a way to share this knowledge with my children, my family, my friends, my loved ones, and with anyone else who cares to use it. Although I'll never be finished looking back, it is with great excitement that I now look to the future. I stand on the threshold, eager for the next step, ready to dive headlong into the second half of my life.

At this point in time, I have no real formula, nothing that I can write down and say, "This is what happened and how it happened" or "This is what I did." As I finish these memoirs, I know that I will continue to write my thoughts, through books, songs, and speeches. This is a new beginning for me.

I am excited about my life, and I am looking forward to my future. I miss my mother deeply, but I know she still lives on in my heart. Time is very important to me; I want to spend more of it with those I love. I love my family so very much: my husband, his three children, his mother, my five children, my father, my sisters and brothers. I have been truly blessed to be a part of the lives of so many: all of my close friends whom I cannot name individually in this book, my work associates, the businesspeople who have taught me, my staff who help and support me in my career and my life, and of course the people who love and buy my music. Most of all, I wish to thank God for everything, especially for the sound of my voice and for my love and caring.

To my readers and listeners, this book and my music are my offerings. When you read my words and listen to my voice, you take a piece of me with you. To all of you, I want you to know that I love you very much. The blessing that I have had in my life, I wish for each of you.

Lifeline: Music, Music, and More Music

1944	Diana Ross born.	Mar. 26
1959	*Tears of Sorrow* — first Primettes single.	Mar.
1961	The Supremes sign with Motown.	Jan. 15
	I Want a Guy — first Supremes single.	Mar. 9
	Buttered Popcorn (single).	Jul. 21
1962	Diana Ross graduates Cass Technical High School.	Jan.
	Your Heart Belongs to Me — first Supremes single released under the Motown label.	May 8
	Let Me Go the Right Way (single).	Nov. 5
1963	*My Heart Can't Take It No More* (single) released.	Feb. 2
	Diana Ross celebrates her 19th birthday.	Mar. 26
	A Breathtaking, First Sight Soul Shaking, One Night Love Making, Next Day Heartbreaking Guy (later shortened to *A Breathtaking Guy*) (single).	June 12
	When the Lovelight Starts Shining Through His Eyes (single) — the first Supremes record to hit the charts.	Oct. 31
	Meet the Supremes, the group's first album, released.	Dec. 9
1964	*Run, Run, Run* (single).	Feb. 7
	Where Did Our Love Go (single) becomes the Supremes' first #1 record.	June 17
	Where Did Our Love Go (album).	Aug. 31
	Baby Love (single; became #1).	Sept. 17
	A Bit of Liverpool (album).	Oct. 16
	Come See About Me (single; became #1).	Oct. 27
	The Supremes make their first TV appearance on *The Ed Sullivan Show*.	Dec. 27
1965	*Hullabaloo* (TV).	Jan. 26
	Stop! In the Name of Love (single; became #1).	Feb. 8
	The Hollywood Palace (TV).	Feb. 27

Funny How Time Slips Away (single) from **The Supremes Sing Country, Western & Pop** (album).	Mar. 22
You Send Me (single) from **We Remember Sam Cooke** (album).	Apr. 12
Back in My Arms Again (single; became #1).	Apr. 15
Things Are Changing (single) released by the U.S. Congress for an Equal Employment Opportunity campaign.	June
Nothing but Heartaches (single).	Jul. 16
More Hits by the Supremes (album).	Jul. 23
The Tonight Show — first appearance (TV).	Jul. 28
The Hollywood Palace.	Aug. 26
Hullabaloo.	Sept. 13
I Hear a Symphony (single; became #1).	Oct. 6
The Ed Sullivan Show.	Oct. 10
Hullabaloo.	Oct. 18
The Supremes at the Copa (album).	Nov. 1
Motown releases *Children's Christmas Song* (single) from **Merry Christmas** (album).	Nov. 18
Hullabaloo.	Dec. 13
My World Is Empty Without You (single).	Dec. 29
Orange Bowl Parade.	Dec. 31
1966 **I Hear a Symphony** (album).	Feb. 18
The Ed Sullivan Show.	Feb. 20
The Sammy Davis Jr. Show (TV).	Mar. 4
The Dean Martin Show (TV).	Mar. 24
Love Is Like an Itching in My Heart (single).	Apr. 8
The Ed Sullivan Show (TV).	May 1
The *Today* show (TV).	June 30
The Ed Sullivan Show.	July 24
You Can't Hurry Love (single; became #1).	July 25
The Tonight Show.	Aug. 18
Supremes A Go-Go (album).	Aug. 25
The Ed Sullivan Show.	Sept. 25
You Keep Me Hangin' On (single; became #1).	Oct. 12
The Hollywood Palace.	Oct. 29
The Ed Sullivan Show.	Dec. 4

1967 *Love Is Here and Now You're Gone* (single; became #1).   Jan. 11

The Andy Williams Show (TV).   Jan. 22

Supremes Sing Holland-Dozier-Holland (album).   Jan. 23

Highlights of Ice Capades '67 (TV special).   Feb. 13

The Happening (single; became #1), from the motion picture   Mar. 20
of the same name.

The Ed Sullivan Show.   May 7

Falling in Love with Love (single) from **The Supremes Sing**   May 22
Rodgers & Hart (album) is released to disc jockeys only.
Also, the May 22 *Tonight Show* telecast is Florence Ballard's
last as a Supreme.

Reflections, the first single released under the new name: Jul. 24
Diana Ross and the Supremes.

Diana Ross and the Supremes   Aug. 29
Greatest Hits Volumes I and II (album).

The Hollywood Palace.   Sept. 25

In and Out of Love (single).   Oct. 25

The Ed Sullivan Show.   Nov. 19

The Tennessee Ernie Ford Special (TV).   Dec. 3

1968 The Supremes guest-star on *Tarzan,* "The Convert" episode (TV).   Jan. 12

The Supremes in Berlin (TV).   Jan. 14

Forever Came Today (single).   Feb. 29

The Ed Sullivan Show.   Mar. 24

Reflections (album).   Mar. 25

During this period, America mourns the loss of the Reverend   Apr. 5
Dr. Martin Luther King, Jr. The day following his assassination
the Supremes perform a beautiful rendition of the song
Somewhere on *The Tonight Show* that includes a memorable
soliloquy that reads, in part: "Let our efforts be as determined as
that of Dr. Martin Luther King, who had a dream..."

The Hollywood Palace.   May 4

The Ed Sullivan Show.   May 5

Some Things You Never Get Used To (single). This song marks   May 21
the beginning of Diana Ross's collaborative efforts with
writers-producers Ashford and Simpson.

Diana Ross and the Supremes, at the request of Coretta Scott   June 19
King, headline a benefit concert at the Atlanta Civic Center
for the Poor People's Campaign.

The Ed Sullivan Show.   June 30

Diana Ross and the Supremes endorse Vice President Hubert Humphrey's presidential bid in New York City.	Jul. 23
The Ed Sullivan Show.	Aug. 18
Diana Ross and the Supremes Sing and Perform "Funny Girl" (album).	Aug. 26
Diana Ross and the Supremes Live at London's Talk of the Town (album).	Aug. 26
Dick Clark and a Cast of Thousands (TV special).	Sept. 6
Love Child (single; became #1). Diana Ross and the Supremes debut this song on *The Ed Sullivan Show.*	Sept. 30
The Bing Crosby Show (TV).	Oct. 23
Love Child (album).	Nov. 8
Diana Ross and the Supremes appear in the Royal Variety Show before Queen Elizabeth II and members of the royal family, the first Motown act given this honor. They sing their rendition of **Somewhere** with the Martin Luther King monologue and receive a resounding ovation.	Nov. 21
Diana Ross and the Supremes Join the Temptations (album).	Nov. 8
I'm Gonna Make You Love Me (single), with the Temptations.	Nov. 21
T.C.B. — Takin' Care of Business (album), with the Temptations.	Dec. 2
T.C.B. TV special broadcast by NBC.	Dec. 9
Diana Ross and the Supremes host *The Hollywood Palace.*	Dec. 28

1969	**I'm Livin' in Shame** (single).	Jan. 6
	The Bob Hope Special (TV).	Feb. 17
	I'll Try Something New (single), with the Temptations.	Feb. 20
	The Hollywood Palace.	Mar. 8
	The Tonight Show.	Mar. 18
	The Composer (single).	Mar. 25
	Like Hep, Diana Ross's first solo TV appearance, with Lucille Ball and Dinah Shore.	Apr. 4
	No Matter What Sign You Are (single).	May 9
	The Ed Sullivan Show.	May 11
	Let the Sunshine In (album).	May 26
	Diana Ross and the Supremes host *The Hollywood Palace.*	May 31
	The Ed Sullivan Show.	Aug. 3
	The Weight (single), with the Temptations.	Aug. 21
	The Ed Sullivan Show.	Sept. 7

Diana Ross guest-stars on *Laugh-In* (TV).	Sept. 22
Together (album), with the Temptations.	Sept. 23
Someday We'll Be Together (single; became #1).	Oct. 14
Diana Ross and the Supremes host *The Hollywood Palace*.	Oct. 18
Cream of the Crop (album).	Nov. 3
The Tonight Show.	Nov. 11
Diana Ross and the Supremes and the Temptations star in their second special together, *G.I.T. on Broadway,* for NBC; soundtrack album released same month.	Nov. 12
Diana Ross makes her final appearance with the Supremes on the *The Ed Sullivan Show*. During this period, Motown releases **Diana Ross and the Supremes, Greatest Hits, Volume 3.**	Dec. 18

1970	Supremes' last appearance together, at the Frontier Hotel.	Jan. 14
	Dick Clark broadcasts video footage of the **Farewell** show on *American Bandstand* (TV).	Feb. 14
	Reach Out and Touch (Somebody's Hand), Diana Ross's first solo single. During this month, Motown releases the album **Farewell,** the final performance of Diana Ross and the Supremes, captured live January 14.	Apr. 6
	Diana Ross (album).	June 19
	Ain't No Mountain High Enough (single; became #1, later nominated for a Grammy Award).	Jul. 16
	The Merv Griffin Show (TV).	Oct. 1
	Everything Is Everything (single and album).	Nov. 3
	Remember Me (single).	Dec. 8

1971	Marries Robert Ellis Silberstein.	Jan. 20
	Guest-stars on *Make Room For Granddaddy* with Danny Thomas (TV).	Feb. 4
	Diana! (original TV special soundtrack).	Mar. 29
	Rona Barrett Report (TV).	Apr. 2
	Diana, first solo TV special, premieres on ABC. In April, Motown releases two Diana Ross singles. The first, **Feelin' Alright,** culled from her first TV special, features Diana Ross and the Jackson 5. The second, **Reach Out, I'll Be There,** is later included on **Surrender.**	Apr. 18
	Surrender (single and album).	July 6
	Rhonda Suzanne is born.	Aug. 14
	I'm Still Waiting (single).	Oct. 13

Principal photography for *Lady Sings the Blues* begins.   Dec. 6

Diana Ross is voted Number One Female Vocalist by *Billboard*,   Dec.
Entertainer of the Year by the NAACP, and Honorary Chairman
of the Image Awards Presentation, and Best TV Special
of the Year is awarded for *Diana!*

1972   Tracee Joy is born.   Oct. 29

Lady Sings the Blues, original motion picture soundtrack, #1.   Nov. 9
The album sold 300,000 copies during the first eight days of its
release. The film was released in October.

The Tonight Show.   Nov. 10

The *Today* show.   Dec. 8

Motown releases a single from **Lady Sings the Blues,**   Dec. 18
Good Morning Heartache.

1973   Provides the half-time entertainment at the Rose Bowl,   Jan. 1
where she sings *Our Love Is Here to Stay*.

The Mike Douglas Show (TV).   Jan. 11

Attends the annual Golden Globe Awards ceremony,   Jan. 28
where she receives the Best Newcomer Award.

The Dick Cavett Show (TV).   Mar. 1

The Tonight Show.   Mar. 1

Jack Paar Tonite (TV).   Mar. 5

Your Choice for the Oscars. This program is a public-   Mar. 18
opinion-poll TV show that asks the public whom it would
select for the year's Academy Awards. Diana Ross is chosen
for Best Actress for her performance as Billie Holiday
in *Lady Sings the Blues.*

Attends Academy Awards ceremony; has been   Mar. 27
nominated for an Oscar for Best Actress for *Lady Sings the Blues.*

Touch Me in the Morning (single; became #1).   May 3

Touch Me in the Morning (album).   June 22

You're a Special Part of Me (single), with Marvin Gaye.   Sept. 13

Diana Ross and Marvin Gaye (album).   Oct. 26

Last Time I Saw Him (single and album).   Dec. 6

By the end of 1973, *Lady Sings the Blues* had received three NAACP
Image Awards and Diana Ross had received, among other accolades
and nominations, *Cue* magazine's Entertainer of the Year Award.

1974   **My Mistake Was to Love You** (single), with Marvin Gaye,   Jan. 17
reaches Top 20 Pop/Top 10 R&B charts.

Cohosts the Academy Awards ceremony.   Apr. 2

Sleepin' (single).	Apr. 4
Yesterday — Good Ol' Rock and Roll (TV special).	Apr. 28
Live! At Caesars Palace (album).	May 15
Don't Knock My Love (single), with Marvin Gaye.	June 18
Principal photography for *Mahogany* begins.	Nov.

1975	*Sorry Doesn't Always Make It Right* (single).	Feb. 11
	Cohosts Don Kirshner's *Rock Music Awards Show* (TV).	Aug. 9
	**The Theme from Mahogany (*Do You Know Where You're Going To?)* (single; became #1).	Sept. 24
	Mahogany (original motion picture soundtrack).	Oct.
	Performs **The Theme from Mahogany** on *The Tonight Show*.	Oct. 3
	Highlights of a Quarter Century of Broadcasting (TV special).	Oct. 24
	The Theme from Mahogany #1 on Billboard's Pop chart.	Nov. 1
	Chudney Lane is born.	Nov. 4

1976	**Diana Ross** released. This album goes on to become a Top 10 Pop and R&B smash hit.	Feb. 10
	I Thought It Took a Little Time (But Today I Fell in Love) (single).	Feb. 20
	Florence Ballard passes away.	Feb. 22
	Love Hangover (single). By June 5 this single is #1 on the Pop, R&B, and Dance charts.	Mar. 16
	Performs the Academy Award–nominated song **The Theme from Mahogany** live via satellite from Holland for the Oscar telecast. This stunning performance is the first of its kind for the Academy Awards broadcast.	Mar. 29
	Diana Ross, Greatest Hits (album). **One Love in My Lifetime** from this album debuts on the charts.	Jul. 12
	Cohosts the Second Annual Rock Awards with Alice Cooper, where she is given *Billboard*'s Female Entertainer of the Century Award.	Sept. 18
	The First Fifty Years of NBC Broadcasting (TV special).	Nov. 21
	Hosts *The Midnight Special* (TV).	Nov. 26

1977	**An Evening with Diana Ross.** This live recording of Diana Ross's one-woman show was recorded at the Ahmanson Theatre in Los Angeles in Sept. 1976. This show ran on Broadway at the Palace Theatre in June 1976, breaking box-office records that had been standing for over 63 years. This same show was developed into a 90-minute television special for NBC, which premiered March 6 and went on to be nominated for numerous Emmy Awards.	Jan. 18

	Performs **The Lady Is a Tramp** on *The Tonight Show*.	Mar. 3
	Baby It's Me (album). In Oct. **Gettin' Ready for Love** (single) from this album is released. Also during this period, Diana Ross goes before the cameras at the Kaufman Astoria Studios in Queens, New York, to begin filming the *The Wiz*.	Sept. 16
	NBC — The First 50 Years: A Closer Look (TV special).	Oct. 23
1978	**Your Love Is So Good for Me** (single) from **Baby It's Me**.	Jan. 24
	You Got It (single) from **Baby It's Me.**	Apr. 13
	Ease On Down the Road (single), with Michael Jackson.	Aug. 21
	Top of the World (single).	Sept. 16
	The Wiz (original motion picture soundtrack).	Sept. 18
	Debuts a spectacular new show in Los Angeles at the Universal Amphitheatre.	Sept. 19
	Dick Clark introduces a live TV broadcast that Diana Ross helps him launch by opening the show with a stellar performance of her smash hit **Ain't No Mountain High Enough.**	Sept. 20
	Motown releases **Ross** (album).	Sept. 21
	The Wiz is launched with a gala premiere in New York.	Oct. 24
	The *Today* show.	Oct. 25
	America Alive! (TV).	Oct. 26
	Diana Ross is profiled on TV for a Barbara Walters special.	Nov. 29
	What You Gave Me (single) from **Ross** is released. Also, Motown releases **Pops We Love You** (single). Diana Ross, Stevie Wonder, Marvin Gaye, and Smokey Robinson recorded this song in honor of Berry Gordy Sr.'s 90th birthday. The record went on to become the Fathers' Day Song of the Year.	Dec. 28
1979	Presents the Best Actor Oscar to Jon Voight at the Academy Awards ceremony.	Apr. 9
	The Boss (album).	May 22
	Hosts *The Tonight Show*.	Jul. 16
	It's My House (single) from **The Boss**.	Oct. 12
	Interviewed by Tom Brokaw on the *Today* show.	Nov. 15
	Sings **The Boss** atop the Big Apple float in Macy's 53rd annual Thanksgiving Day Parade. On the same day Bryant Gumbel presents Diana Ross with the New York *Daily News* Front Page Music Award.	Nov. 22
1980	*Sensational Wacky Seventies* (TV special).	Jan. 4
	Appears on *The Muppet Show* with Kermit and Miss Piggy (TV).	May 19
	Bob Hope's All-Star Comedy Birthday Party: A USO Salute (TV).	May 28

diana. From this platinum album, Motown releases	May 22	
Upside Down, which became #1, and	June 20	
I'm Coming Out.	Aug. 22	
It's My Turn, the title song from the motion picture of the same name.	Sept. 29	
The Wiz — television premiere.	Oct. 11	
1981 HBO broadcasts Diana Ross's first made-for-cable special, *Standing Room Only: Diana Ross.* This telecast contains elements of Diana Ross's spectacular show that debuted in Los Angeles in 1978.	Jan. 13	
To Love Again. This album is a compilation of Diana Ross's work with writer/producer Michael Masser.	Feb. 17	
Good Morning America (TV).	Feb. 25	
Motown releases **One More Chance** from **To Love Again.**	Feb. 27	
Good Morning America (TV).	Feb. 25	
CBS broadcasts *diana*, a special that contains live concert footage that was taped Feb. 5 at the Los Angeles Forum.	Mar. 2	
Attends the Academy Awards ceremony with Michael Jackson.	Mar. 31	
Cryin' My Heart Out for You (single).	May 8	
Signs with RCA Records.	May 14	
Endless Love (single; became #1), with Lionel Richie. This title song from the motion picture soundtrack goes on to top the charts for a record-breaking nine weeks. It is nominated for Grammys in several categories, including Song of the Year, Record of the Year, and Best Pop Duo. It is also nominated by the Academy of Motion Pictures Arts and Sciences for Song of the Year.	June 24	
Why Do Fools Fall In Love (single; became #1). Both the single and album are released the same month. This is Diana Ross's first package for RCA. She has produced it herself, and the album goes platinum. Motown issues its own albums the same month, **All the Greatest Hits** and **Diana's Duets.**	Sept. 25	
Good Morning America.	Oct. 23	
Good Morning America.	Oct. 26	
It's My Turn, original motion picture soundtrack.	Oct. 29	
20/20 (TV).	Oct. 29	
Motown releases *My Old Piano* (single).	Dec. 4	
Mirror, Mirror (single).	Dec. 11	
The Tonight Show.	Dec. 11	
1982 Sings the National Anthem at Super Bowl XVI.	Jan. 24	
Soul Train (TV).	Jan. 30	

	Work That Body (single).	Mar. 19
	At the Academy Awards ceremony, Diana Ross and Lionel Richie perform ***Endless Love***, which has been nominated for Best Song.	Mar. 29
	The *Today* show.	June 14
	Good Morning America.	July 1
	Diana Ross performs at Meadowland Stadium in East Rutherford, New Jersey. The guests she selects to share the evening with her are jazz great Miles Davis and R&B group Frankie Beverly and Maze.	July 4
	Motown issues ***We Can Never Light That Flame Again*** (single).	Aug. 31
	Silk Electric (album).	Sept. 10
	Muscles, a tune penned by Michael Jackson, is the first single released from **Silk Electric.** It goes on to become a Top 10 Pop and R&B hit, and earns Diana Ross yet another Grammy nomination, for Best Female R&B Vocalist.	Sept. 17
1983	***So Close*** (single).	Jan. 7
	Anthology (album).	May 5
	Takes part in the Emmy Award–winning *Motown 25—Yesterday, Today & Forever* (TV special).	May 16
	Ross (RCA album).	June 17
	Pieces of Ice, the first single from **Ross,** is released.	June 17
	Bill Harris in Hollywood, interview with Diana Ross, airs on Showtime (TV).	Jul.
	Bryant Gumbel interviews Diana Ross on the *Today* show.	Jul. 20, 21
	"For One and For All—Diana Ross Live! in Central Park." Diana Ross performs before 800,000 people in a free concert in Central Park, New York City.	Jul. 21, 22
	Performs ***Let's Go Up*** on *The Tonight Show.*	Aug. 4
	Launches 45-city concert tour.	Aug. 5
	Up Front (single).	Sept.
	Let's Go Up (single) from **Ross.**	Nov. 18
1984	***All of You*** (single), with Julio Iglesias.	June 20
	Swept Away (single and album).	Aug. 2
	Performs ***Forever Young*** for Jerry Lewis's muscular dystrophy telethon.	Sept. 3
	Diana Ross's Radio City Music Hall show breaks box-office records.	Sept. 19
	Diana Ross's mother, Ernestine Ross-Jordan, passes away.	Oct. 9
	Missing You (single); becomes a #1 R&B and #10 Pop record.	Nov. 16

1985   Kaufman Astoria Studios in Queens, New York, names   Jan. 24
a building after Diana Ross in recognition of her contributions
to reviving the New York film industry.

Is a special guest presenter at the American Music Awards.   Jan. 28
Following this presentation, Diana Ross goes to the A&M
Studios in Hollywood to participate in the recording of a song
that would become a #1 record around the world,
We Are the World.

Performs at the Apollo Theatre for *Motown Returns to the*   May 4
Apollo (TV special).

Telephone (single), from **Swept Away**.   June 3

Eaten Alive (album).   Aug.23

Chain Reaction (single), from **Eaten Alive**.   Oct. 25

1986   Performs at Kennedy Center in Washington, D.C.,   Jan. 20
for Martin Luther King Day celebration.

Hosts the 13th annual American Music Awards.   Jan. 27

Marries Arne Naess in Switzerland.   Feb. 1

Ground-breaking ceremony for the Diana Ross   Sept. 11
Playground at 81st Street and Central Park West.

1987   Hosts the 14th annual American Music Awards.   Jan. 27

Dirty Looks (album).   Apr. 29

Red Hot Rhythm and Blues TV special airs on ABC.   May 20

Red Hot Rhythm and Blues album released.   June 9

Tell Me Again (single).   July

Ross Arne is born.   Oct. 7

1988   Attends Grammy Awards ceremony in New York and   Mar. 2
presents U2 with the Album of the Year Award.

Evan Olav is born.   Aug.26

If We Hold On Together (single), from Steven Spielberg's   Nov. 5
animated film *The Land Before Time,* is released on MCA Records.

1989   Embarks on world tour.   Feb. 1

Re-signs with Motown.   Feb. 10

Workin' Overtime (single).   Apr. 24

Workin' Overtime (album).   May 24

Participates in Our Common Future, an ecological   June 23
awareness concert internationally simulcast from
Wembley, England.

1990	Attends the Academy Awards ceremony with her daughters and performs Harold Arlen's *Somewhere over the Rainbow*.	Mar. 26
	Daughter Tracee Ross graduates from high school. Diana Ross gives commencement address.	June 13
	No Matter What You Do, with Al B. Sure, is released on Sure's Warner Bros. album **Private Times and the Whole 9!**	Oct. 16
	Diana Ross and daughter Tracee model Thierry Mugler's 1991 spring collection in Paris.	Oct. 18
1991	Presents Record of the Year Grammy to Phil Collins.	Feb. 20
	Debuts the Stevie Wonder song *The Force Behind the Power* on *The Arsenio Hall Show* (TV).	May 20
	Begins a 15-month world tour to promote her new album **The Force Behind the Power.** Singles released from this disc include *When You Tell Me,* which Diana Ross performs on *The Tonight Show*.	May 31 Jul. 23
1992	Diana Ross performs an entire evening of jazz and blues at the Ritz in New York City, live, for pay-per-view TV: **"Diana Ross Live/The Lady Sings Jazz & Blues, Stolen Moments."**	Dec. 4
	On the *Christmas in Vienna* TV special, Diana Ross performs Christmas classics with Placido Domingo and Jose Carreras.	Dec. 23
1993	*When You Dream,* children's book and CD, Japanese edition.	Apr.
	Daughter Rhonda Ross graduates from college with honors.	May 31
	Receives Global Youth Forum Award at U.N.	June 3
	Daughter Chudney Ross graduates from high school. Diana Ross gives commencement address.	June 10
	Performs Billie Holiday classics on *Apollo Theatre Hall of Fame* (live TV).	June 15
	Principal photography begins on *Out of Darkness*, ABC TV movie.	Aug. 3

Permission
Acknowledgments

Grateful acknowledgment is made to the following for permission to reprint previously published material:

C AND B WEST PUBLISHING, CO.: Four lines from "Tears of Sorrow" by Richard Morris. Reprinted by permission of C and B West Publishing, Co.

JOAN DAVES AGENCY: An excerpt from "I Have a Dream" by Martin Luther King, Jr. Copyright 1963 by Martin Luther King, Jr. Copyright renewed 1991 by Coretta Scott King. Reprinted by arrangement with the heirs to the Estate of Martin Luther King, Jr., c/o Joan Daves Agency as agent for the proprietor.

EMI MUSIC PUBLISHING AND WARNER/CHAPPELL MUSIC, INC.: Three lines from "It's My Turn" by Michael Masser and Carole Bayer Sager. © 1980 by Colgems-EMI Music Inc., Prince Street Music, Unichappell Music Inc. and Begonia Melodies Inc. All rights on behalf of Prince Street Music controlled and administered by Colgems-EMI Music Inc. All rights reserved. International copyright secured. Used by permission.

JOBETE MUSIC CO., INC.: Nine lines from "Ain't No Mountain High Enough" by Nicholas Ashford and Valerie Simpson. Copyright © 1967 by Jobete Music Co., Inc.; and five lines from "Buttered Popcorn" by Berry Gordy and Barney Ales. Copyright © 1961 by Jobete Music Co., Inc. Reprinted by permission of Jobete Music Co., Inc.

WARNER/CHAPPELL MUSIC, INC.: Ten lines from "Home" by Charlie Smalls. © 1974 by Warner-Tamerlane Publishing Corp. All rights reserved. Used by permission.

Photo Credits

Grateful acknowledgment is made to the following for permission to reprint photographs. Every reasonable effort has been made to trace the ownership of all photographs included in this volume. Any errors that may have occurred are inadvertent, and will be corrected in subsequent editions provided notification is sent to the publisher.

New York

PAGE 1, TOP TO BOTTOM: AP/Wide World Photos; Joe McNally; AP/Wide World Photos.

Caught in the Act

PAGE 2: Joe McNally.

PAGE 13: Wildenberg/Sygma.

The Face in the Mirror

PAGE 14, LEFT: AP/Wide World Photos; RIGHT: UPI/Bettman.

Detroit

PAGE 23: All photos personal photos from the Diana Ross Collection.

Mama, I Miss You

PAGE 24: Personal photo from the Diana Ross Collection.

PAGE 31: Personal photo from the Diana Ross Collection.

A Quiet Force

PAGE 32: Personal photo from the Diana Ross Collection.

Sweet Like Jelly

PAGE 36: Personal photo from the Diana Ross Collection.

5736 St. Antoine

PAGE 40: Personal photo from the Diana Ross Collection.

A Bad Dream

PAGE 44: Personal photo from the Diana Ross Collection.

PAGE 47: Personal photo from the Diana Ross Collection.

Just Let Yo' Ole Curtains Burn Up!

PAGE 48: Personal photo from the Diana Ross Collection.

Big-Screen Magic

PAGE 52: Personal photo from the Diana Ross Collection.

PAGE 55: Personal photo from the Diana Ross Collection.

A Wailing Night
PAGE 56: Personal photo from the Diana Ross Collection.
PAGE 59: Personal photo from the Diana Ross Collection.

Fighting Back
PAGE 60: Personal photo from the Diana Ross Collection.

Point of Origin
PAGES 64–65: All photos personal photos from the Diana Ross Collection.

I Sing Because I'm Happy
PAGE 66: Photofest.

Under the African Skies
PAGE 70: Personal photo from the Diana Ross Collection.

Down and Dirty
PAGE 80: Chuck Pulin/Starfile.

Reflections of . . .
PAGE 86: All photos personal photos from the Diana Ross Collection.
PAGE 87 (CLOCKWISE FROM TOP LEFT): Art Shay; personal photo from the Diana Ross Collection; Motown Records Archives; Motown Museum Archives, Detroit.

The Primettes
PAGE 88: Motown Records Archives.

Buttered Popcorn
PAGE 98: Art Shay.
PAGE 109: Personal photo from the Diana Ross Collection.

Those Good Old Dreams
PAGE 110: Poster from the Diana Ross Collection.

Get Up and Sit on the Piano
PAGE 120: Photo from the R. Lash Collection.

Going Through Changes
PAGE 132: Motown Records album cover.

A Wild Ride
PAGE 138: Both photos from the Motown Museum Archives, Detroit.

Days of Rage
PAGE 146: Paul Fusco/Magnum Photos.
PAGE 151: Personal photo from the Diana Ross Collection.

"Someday We'll Be Together"
PAGE 152: Photo from the Sharon Davis Collection.
PAGE 157: Personal photo from the Diana Ross Collection.

Distance Traveled

Pages 158–59 (clockwise from top left): Frank Griffen/Image Equity Management, Inc.; Frank Griffen/Image Equity Management, Inc.; David Lissy; Frank Griffen/Image Equity Management, Inc.; personal photo from the Diana Ross Collection; Robin Platzer/Twin Images; personal photo from the Diana Ross Collection.

Through the Blues

Page 160: Michel Comte/Image Equity Management, Inc.

Ross Goods

Page 172, top to bottom: Skrebneski; Skrebneski; Harry Langdon/Image Equity Management, Inc.

Learning to Fly

Page 178: Herb Ritts/Image Equity Management, Inc.

Page 183: Douglas Kirkland/Image Equity Management, Inc.

A Strange Wind

Page 184: Douglas Kirkland/Image Equity Management, Inc.

Hello, World

Page 192: Michel Comte/Image Equity Management, Inc.

Page 199: Douglas Kirkland/Image Equity Management, Inc.

It's My Turn

Page 200: Skrebneski.

Page 209: Douglas Kirkland/Image Equity Management, Inc.

The Magical Light of Dusk

Page 210: Skrebneski.

Interiors

Page 219: All photos personal photos from the Diana Ross Collection.

Still Places

Page 220: Albert Watson/Image Equity Management, Inc.

Light over Darkness

Page 226: Herb Ritts/Image Equity Management, Inc.

Standing Tall Through It All

Page 230: Michel Comte/Image Equity Management, Inc.

Page 235: Hurrell/Image Equity Management, Inc.

Full Circle

Page 236: Mark Abrams/Image Equity Management, Inc.

Weaving the Tapestry

Page 241: All photos personal photos from the Diana Ross Collection.

A Private Life

Page 242: Painting by Aaron Shikler from the Diana Ross Collection.

Goose Bumps

Page 250: Personal photo from the Diana Ross Collection.

Antique Lace
PAGE 260: Personal photo from the Diana Ross Collection.

Thinking of a Rainbow
PAGE 264: Illustration by Debbie Ani/Image Equity Management, Inc.

Snow Crystals
PAGE 270: Personal photo from the Diana Ross Collection.

Miracles
PAGE 276: The White House.

Photo insert following page 142
PAGE 1: Motown Records Archives
PAGE 2 (CLOCKWISE FROM TOP LEFT): Art Shay; Sharon Davis Collection; personal photo from the Diana Ross Collection; Art Shay.
PAGE 3 (CLOCKWISE FROM TOP LEFT): Art Shay; personal photo from the Diana Ross Collection; personal photo from the Diana Ross Collection; Topham Picture Source.
PAGE 4: Harry Langdon/Motown Records Archives.
PAGE 5: Harry Langdon/Motown Records Archives.
PAGE 6 (CLOCKWISE FROM TOP LEFT): R. Lash Collection; R. Lash Collection; Photofest.
PAGE 7 (CLOCKWISE FROM TOP LEFT): Archive Photos/Frank Driggs; R. Lash Collection; Photofest.
PAGE 8: Motown Records Archives.

Photo insert following page 206
PAGE 1: Harry Langdon, from the Diana Ross Collection.
PAGE 2: All photos personal photos from the Diana Ross Collection.
PAGE 3: All photos personal photos from the Diana Ross Collection, except second down from top left: Charles Bush/Sygma.
PAGE 4 (CLOCKWISE FROM TOP): Robin Platzer/Twin Images; personal photo from the Diana Ross Collection; personal photo from the Diana Ross Collection; illustration from the birth announcement of Chudney Lane Silberstein.
PAGE 5 (CLOCKWISE FROM TOP LEFT): Personal photo from the Diana Ross Collection; George Hurell, from the Diana Ross Collection; all other photos personal photos from the Diana Ross Collection.
PAGE 6 (CLOCKWISE FROM TOP LEFT): Skrebneski; illustration from the Diana Ross Collection; personal photo from the Diana Ross Collection; Robin Platzer/Twin Images; all other photos Orlando-Paramount Pictures, Inc.
PAGE 7 (CLOCKWISE FROM TOP LEFT): Personal photo from the Diana Ross Collection; personal photo from the Diana Ross Collection; personal photo from the Diana Ross Collection; personal photo from the Diana Ross Collection; Motown Records Archive Photos/Frank Driggs; Globe Photos; Motown Records Archives; personal photo from the Diana Ross Collection.
PAGE 8: Peter C. Borsari.

Photo insert (color) following page 238
PAGE 1: Herb Ritts/Image Equity Management, Inc.
PAGE 2: Marco Glavino.
PAGE 3: Douglas Kirkland/Motown Records Archives.

PAGE 4: Eddie Wolf/Image Equity Management, Inc.

PAGE 5: Eddie Wolf/Image Equity Management, Inc.

PAGE 6: Harry Langdon/Image Equity Management, Inc.

PAGE 7: Aller Group, Norway.

PAGE 8: Personal photo from the Diana Ross Collection.

Photo insert following page 270

PAGE 1: Albert Watson/Image Equity Management, Inc.

PAGE 2: All photos personal photos from the Diana Ross Collection.

PAGE 3: All photos personal photos from the Diana Ross Collection, except bottom photo, Herb Ritts/The Gap, Inc.

PAGE 4: All photos personal photos from the Diana Ross Collection.

PAGE 5: All photos personal photos from the Diana Ross Collection.

PAGE 6: Albert Watson/Image Equity Management, Inc.

PAGE 7: Albert Watson/Image Equity Management, Inc.

PAGE 8: Albert Watson/Image Equity Management, Inc.

Endpapers

Photographs of endpaper tableaux by Scott Starr.

FRONT ENDPAPER (CLOCKWISE FROM TOP LEFT): Poster from the Diana Ross Collection; Art Shay; personal photo from the Diana Ross Collection; Sharon Davis Collection; button and two posters from the R. Lash Collection.

BACK ENDPAPER (CLOCKWISE FROM TOP LEFT): Personal photo from the Diana Ross Collection; Harry Langdon/Image Equity Management, Inc.; Douglas Kirkland/Motown Records Archives; Harry Langdon/Image Equity Management, Inc.; Harry Langdon/Image Equity Management, Inc.